Blast Off to Reading!

50 Orton-Gillingham Based Lessons
for Struggling Readers and Those with Dyslexia

by Cheryl Orlassino

Blast Off to Learning Press

Check out our decodable **chapter books** for dyslexic students!
These books are designed to foster independent reading, having a story
to interest older children, but with short sentences and
paragraphs with simpler text.
Comprehension worksheets available!

For information, apps, phonics tools and chapter books, go to
www.BlastOffToLearningPress.com

Published By Blast Off to Learning Press
New York

e-mail all inquiries to:
contact@BlastOffToLearningPress.com

Printed in the United States of America
ISBN: 978-0-9831996-3-2, REV E (3)

Table of Contents

To the Parent or Instructor

1. This **physical book** contains the *complete* reading program; there are no other components required. To augment the program, there are physical phonics games/tools and a web app available at our site. The web app and the physical games/tools are not part of the sale of this book. The web app is available as a free bonus add-on for those who have purchased the book, and may not work on all devices. In addition, at some future date, the web app may not be updated or may not be available.

2. For tutors and teachers who **instruct remotely**, there is a Kindle Teacher's Manual available. This manual contains instructions for the teacher, slides for presenting the lessons, and all lesson pages from this book. Visit our site for more information (www.BlastOffToLearningPress.com).

3. The success of this program is dependent on the **consistency of instruction**, student focus level, and student memory.

    a) **Consistency of instruction:** It is recommended that this program be done five days a week, two days a week at a minimum. Studies have shown that the faster an intensive reading program is implemented, the more effective it is.

    b) Student **focus level and memory**: Since this program requires understanding and memorizing, if the student has a poor working memory or has ADD/ADHD, the program may take longer. For some, with severe focus problems, this program may not be the correct fit.

4. For **independent reading** (after Lesson 19), we recommend our chapter books, which have interesting stories, for older students, with a lower reading level (approximately a second-grade level).

5. The book is **not intended to teach English Language Arts (ELA);** however, some ELA topics are introduced for decoding purposes. These include: homophones, contractions, and apostrophes for ownership. More work in this area may need to be done, for which there are many other materials available.

6. Throughout the workbook there will be **messages to for the instructor.** These messages are indicated by the image below.

7. For **number/letter reversals**, please go to our website at www.BlastOffToLearningPress, where this is discussed. You will also find

activities that can be done to help remedy reversals. Note that the web app for this reading program contains several activities for reversals.

8. Since this book is meant for a wide range of ages, some words may not be familiar to some students. Try to have the child read these words, and, if receptive, explain the meanings.

9. This program is fluid and is always changing as more experienced is gained. Your thoughts and input would be greatly appreciated. Please email your thoughts and ideas.

10. An **erratum** (a list of corrections) for this printed material can be found at our site. Navigate to this program's web page and scroll to the bottom for the link. If you find errors, please let us know (email: contact@BlastOffToLearningPress.com).

Reading Program Instructions

Before you Begin
If you plan on using the web app for this program, follow the instructions below.

1. Go to www.blastofftoreading.com.
2. If using a tablet or phone, save the page to the home-screen and then reopen the app from the home-screen.
3. Select the image that says, "Select to activate the Blast Off App".
4. Once you accept the Terms & Conditions, you will be asked which version of the book you have. Select Rev E.
5. You will then be asked to look in your book for a word to enter. For example, if it says to enter the word at Exercise 24.1 #5, go to Lesson 24, Exercise 1, then enter the word at #5, "haunt". You will then have access to the web app. You can use more than one device if needed. Note that as per the license agreement, as stated in the Terms & Conditions, there can only be one user per purchased book.
6. If you have trouble, please visit our site for more instructions, troubleshooting, and an instructional video.

Implementing the Program

Work **2 to 5 days a week** with your student(s), for 30 to 45 minutes. This program is best done one-on-one; however, it can also be used in small groups. If working one-on-one, sit on the **same side** of the table as your student (not across from him/her). If you're right-handed, sit to the right of the child, otherwise sit on the left side.

A typical lesson is as follows:

1. Review the flash cards for the sounds & rules.
2. Check your student's dictations.
3. Use the workbook for the lesson (you may be starting a new lesson or continuing a lesson that has not been completed).
4. Play phonics related games and/or read from a book.

In the beginning, depending on the severity of the reading problem, you may need to spend some extra time developing phonemic awareness (connecting the smallest units of sounds together). You can use lowercase letter tiles, magnetic letters, a white board, or the Letter Tiles activity on the web app, to create sounds for practice. *Always use lowercase since this is what most words are comprised of.*

Flash Cards & Phonics Reference Chart

Most lessons introduce new sounds or rules which require review. This repetition is done using flash cards as well as the phonics reference chart (on the back cover of this book). For the flash cards, you can either make your own, purchase them from our site, or use the online version that is included in the web app that accompanies this program.

Review the cards before each lesson. Once a sound or rule is completely mastered, the associated card can be skipped. The phonics reference chart can be used for a quick review, or to reference when your student needs help in identifying a sound.

Dictations

Most lessons require the student to *independently* write words and sentences in a "dictation book". For this, a composition book dedicated for this purpose is recommended. Date the page at the top so you can see how improvement progresses over time.

The dictation lists are included in the back of this book. You can either read the words to your student from the lists, or your student can use the online audio dictations which is included in the web app that accompanies this program.

Dictations (or portions) may have to be repeated if there were many errors. This is left to the instructor's discretion, and dependent on your objectives, time constraints, and your student.

Do not let the student study and memorize the words (unless otherwise noted on the dictations lists). He/she should use the sounds and rules learned to spell the words. When done, correct the work with your student. Have him/her **read the words to you from his/her own handwriting** and write the corrected word next to any that were misspelled, making sure to use the rules learned. There is no need to write the misspelled word over many times.

For the sentences, make sure the student leaves a line or two between the sentences so there is room for corrections. When checking, have the child read the sentences to you from his/her own writing (as done for the words). If a word is misspelled, have him or her sound it out and make the correction. Help when needed. Note that sometimes the student may omit entire words, switch words around or even change a word. This is very common. All corrections should be made on the lines above or below the sentences.

If a letter is reversed, but all else is correct, simply have the child write over the letter and count the word as correct (keep a note of the reversals so you can address them later).

If your main objective in using this program is for reading (not spelling), the dictations become optional at Lesson 37 (this point is indicated in the word lists).

The Workbook Lesson

This workbook contains 50 lessons with a review section after every 10 lessons. Each lesson usually contains a new sound or rule, a review (lists of words and/or sentences) and then exercises.

When you come upon letters inside of slashes, you should say the actual *sound* of the letter(s). Anything in single quotes is meant for you to spell.

Example: If you see /ar/ (in slashes), you should read it as the sound "ar" (as in "jar").
If you see 'ar' (in single quotes), you should read it as the letters "a", "r".

A lesson is not meant to be done in one sitting, although that can happen. Don't rush your student; let him/her do this program at his/her own pace. Each child will be different. The first few lessons may seem very easy for the student, but **do not skip them;** they are extremely important for providing a good foundation for phonemic awareness.

On-Line Tools & Games

If you are using the web app to accompany this program, the lessons will indicate which games should be played. This is done at the end of the lesson (if applicable).

There are two games that can be played with any lesson (except for Lesson 1). They are the *Blast Off Matching Game*, where two players take turns finding matching cards while reading the words on the cards, and the *Save the Earth Reading Game*, which is a fun way to read words (with fun games to play upon completion). These games must be played with another player who is a proficient reader.

Blast Off
Matching Game

Save the Earth
Reading Game

Important Tips

> Since many letter names are different from their actual sounds (such as 'w' – 'double-u'), instruct your student to say (out loud) the letter **sounds** as he or she writes (not the letter names). If *you* are decoding a word to the student, don't say the actual letter names, only say the sounds. Letter names should only be used when introducing a new sound which is comprised of two or more letters, such as the /th/ sound. However, once the sound is introduced, when you see those letters in a word, you should only say the actual *sound*.

> When a student has trouble reading a word, cover it up with your finger and slowly reveal the letters. If the letter needs another letter to make a sound (such as 'th') reveal both letters at one time.

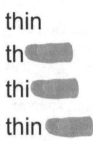

> If you see your student becoming frustrated, slow down and review something else. You don't want to give too much information at one time.

For the Younger Student

For students that are 7 to 8 years old, some concepts taught will exceed what is expected of them at their age. It will be to your discretion how this is to be handled. If your student is receptive and eager, then continue as instructed. However, if you're losing your student, or he/she becomes noncompliant, you may want to stop and review concepts, as well as have him/her read material that is at his/her level, for reinforcement.

Side-by-Side Reading

Once Lesson 19 (long vowels) is complete, it is recommended that the student read books of interest with a proficient reader (PR). To do this, we use The Side-by-Side Reading (or "partnered" reading) method. The importance of this cannot be understated. This is what bridges what was taught in this program to real life application and leads to fluency.

The child and proficient reader (PR) should sit next to each other (facing the same direction). If the PR is right handed, he/she should sit to the right of the child. The PR should use his/her index finger to point to each word, helping the student track and stay focused. When the student struggles with a word, the PR should give some time for the child to work it out. After a few seconds, the PR should ask if the child needs help. Often children want very much to decode the word and worry that the instructor is going to read it for them. On the other hand, many children want to be given the answer so that they don't have to work. If the child needs help, block the sounds in the word, revealing sounds that were taught. If there is a sound in the word that wasn't taught, encourage the student to try to decode it based on context of the sentence and the sounds (s)he can recognize. If your student becomes frustrated, or this takes too long, simply read these words to him or her.

For example, if the word is "strangers", show "ange", "str" and "er". You don't need to do this in order. Sometimes, first showing sounds that are at the end of the word helps. For example: "adventure" – first block out all letters except for 'ture' (which = /chur/).

If the student is reading along, but reads a word incorrectly, the PR should double tap his/her finger. This non-verbal cue doesn't break the flow, and the student will quickly learn what it means.

Often students with dyslexia will take "the wild guess". This is when he or she quickly guesses, incorrectly, the word without decoding based on context. When this is done, the PR should double tap, forcing the student to try again.

If reading is slow and labored, the PR and student should take turns reading paragraphs.

Eventually, the student will read without the finger guidance, and then, in time, he or she will be able to read independently.

NOTE: If you happen to find errors in this book, or you have comments for improvement, please email us at: contact@BlastOffToLearningPress.com.

Consonants & Vowels

Make sure that your student can identify the consonant sounds.
*You will have to work on the troubled consonant sounds separately, and have them mastered before proceeding to the next lesson.

Note that from this point on, until otherwise noted, **'c' and 'g' will always have hard sounds** as in "cat" and "get", and **'y' will have the consonant** sound as in "yellow".

Exercise 1.1

Write the first letter for the words that identifies the pictures.

1. _____

2. _____

3. _____

4. _____

5. _____

6. _____

7. _____

8. _____

9. _____

10. _____

11. _____

12. _____

13. _____

14. _____

15. _____

16. _____

17. _____

18. _____

19. _____

The vowels, as well as 'q' & 'x' are omitted on purpose.

Vowels

The letters below are special. They are called **vowels**.

a e i o u

When an 'a' is **printed**, it usually looks like this:	When an 'a' is **written**, it usually looks like this:
a	a

Vowels have two sounds: **long** sounds and **short** sounds.
The long sound is easy, it's the letter names.
But **short vowels** have special sounds, and we
will use the pictures below to help identify those sounds.

Using the image above, your student should say:
"/ah/ - apple, /eh/ - elephant, /ih/ - igloo,
/oh/ - octopus, /uh/ - umbrella"
Note that phonetic symbols will not be used in this book.
The above image will be on the <u>first flash card</u>.

For consistency, always use these images and/or words
to identify short vowel sounds.

Exercise 1.2
Below is the alphabet. Circle the vowels.

a b c d e f g h i j k l m
n o p q r s t u v w x y z

Exercise 1.3
Draw lines to match the first sound of the pictures to the letters.

1.    a

2. 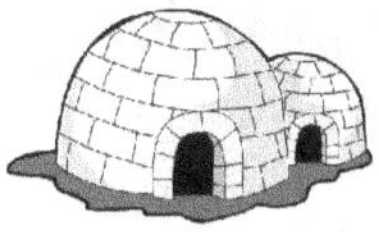   e

3.    i

4.    o

5.    u

Exercise 1.4
Circle the vowel that goes with the beginning sound for each picture below.

1. a e i o u

2. a e i o u

3. a e i o u

4. a e i o u

The pictures above are:
axe, elbow, ostrich, & umpire.

Exercise 1.5
Write the vowel that goes with the pictures below.

1.  ☐   4. ☐

2.  ☐   5.  ☐

3. ☐

Review the flash cards for lesson 1.
Your student should say:
/ah/ - apple, /eh/ - elephant, /ih/ - igloo,
/oh/ - octopus, /uh/ - umbrella

In this lesson we will see combinations
of vowels and consonants.

**Until otherwise instructed,
you should always read 'g' as /g/ as in "get",
and read 'c' as /k/ as in "cat".**

Read the vowel-consonant combinations below. All vowels
are short, so 'no' should be read as /noh/ with a short 'o'.

ta	na	la
te	ne	le
ti	ni	li
to	no	lo
tu	nu	lu

at	an	al
et	en	el
it	in	il
ot	on	ol
ut	un	ul

ca	mo	pa	du	ge	zi	pe
ga	si	ho	fa	co	bo	gu

ac	om	ap	ud	eg	iz	ep
ag	ig	oh	af	oc	ob	ug

Letter & Number Reversals

Very often, students who are dyslexic will reverse the following letters: 'b', 'd', and 'p' . Although other letters and numbers can be reversed, these are the most frequent.

Reversal Games

Make notes of the reversals that each student makes and work on these individually. Note that you can use our on-line games for reversals on the Blast Off Web App.

Reversals can be done when reading and/or writing. Very often when writing, students will substitute the uppercase letter, since those are not usually reversed. For example, they may write "number" as "numBer". This is an indication that they confuse lowercase d' and 'b'.

b-d-p Reversals When Reading

Read the vowel-consonant combinations below.

di	ba	bi
bu	de	pu
po	du	bo

id	ab	ib
ub	ed	up
op	ud	ob

Exercise 2.1

Circle the sound to complete the words.

1.	p_ _	an	in	un
2.	t_ _	ob	ab	ub
3.	b_ _	at	it	ot
4.	f_ _	ax	ix	ox

Exercise 2.2

For each line, circle the word that has a **short** vowel sound.

1.

2.

3.

4.

Exercise 2.3

Circle the sound to complete the words.

1.	n＿＿	et	it	ot
2.	r＿＿	og	ag	ug
3.	h＿＿	an	in	en
4.	m＿＿	in	an	on

High Frequency Words

Below are high frequency words, where most are not spelled the way they sound. See which words your student can read. These will be on the flash cards and should be reviewed until mastered.

me	you	is	who	to
we	your	his	what	of
be	they	said	when	no
he	do	the	where	so
she	does	have	why	go
my	was	has	there	

Exercise 2.4

Read the sentences below to your student using the word "blank" for the underlined word choices. Then have him/her choose and circle the correct words for each sentence.

1. <u>My / Me</u> dog likes to go for a walk.

2. They <u>has / have</u> a black cat.

3. What <u>was / does</u> she looking at?

4. Why <u>does / do</u> they want to go there?

5. She <u>does / said</u> that she likes chocolate.

Exercise 2.5

Read the sentences below to your student using the word "blank" for the underlined word choices. Then have him/her choose and circle the correct words for each sentence.

1. Where are <u>he / you</u> going?

2. Where <u>does / do</u> he live?

3. <u>She / He</u> likes her pink dress.

4. <u>What / Who</u> told you to go?

5. We will <u>go / have</u> home later.

6. <u>What / Where</u> are his shoes?

7. Where are <u>you / your</u> books?

Have your student play the games below for this lesson. The two games below contain word lists for most lessons and should be played as often as possible.

Blast Off
Matching Game

Save the Earth
Reading Game

1) Review the flash cards.

2) Do a warm-up for the VC / CV combinations (as done in the last lesson) using **lowercase** letter tiles, magnetic letters or a moveable alphabet on a device.

Here we have a short vowel in-between two consonants, just like a sandwich!

consonant - vowel - consonant

Read the words below.

top	lap	jab	job
vet	tap	net	pep
ban	bed	mad	set
tax	dig	mix	fat
lag	jet	kin	max
tip	did	lax	pot

Read the nonsense words below.

| sut | pog | bup | dop | gib | dat |
| mig | lun | tud | tid | gid | bom |

Exercise 3.1
Circle the **middle short vowel** sounds for the pictures below.

1.   a   e   i   o   u

2.   a   e   i   o   u

3.   a   e   i   o   u

4.   a   e   i   o   u

5.   a   e   i   o   u

6.   a   e   i   o   u

Exercise 3.2
Fill in the missing short vowels for the words below.

1. 10   t___n

2.   v___n

3.   b___x

4.   m___p

5.   s___n

6.   p___g

Exercise 3.3

Read the following sentences to your student INCLUDING the words in question. Then have him/her choose and circle the correct spelling for the underlined words.

1. What <u>wuz / was</u> the show about?

2. She <u>has / haz</u> a small house.

3. <u>They / Thay</u> are going out to dinner.

4. <u>Whut / What</u> are you eating?

5. Where <u>duz / does</u> he go after school?

Exercise 3.4

Circle the **middle short vowel** sound for the pictures below.

1. a e i o u

2. a e i o u

3. a e i o u

4. a e i o u

5. a e i o u

6. a e i o u

Exercise 3.5
Fill in the missing letters ('b', 'd' or 'p') for the words below.

1.  __ en

2.  __ at

3.  __ug

4.  li__

5. __un

6.  mo__

7.  __ an

8.  tu__

9. __in

10. __og

Exercise 3.6
Read the sentences to your student, inserting the word "blank" for the underlined words, and have him/her circle the words to complete the sentences.

1. Where did _we / my_ dog go?

2. _They / She_ have been waiting in line a long time.

3. He _have / has_ a baseball game tonight.

4. My sister _was / does_ not like spiders.

5. He _was / is_ at my house yesterday.

Exercise 3.7
Circle the **middle short vowel** sound for the pictures below.

1.  a   e   i   o   u

2. a   e   i   o   u

3. a   e   i   o   u

4. a   e   i   o   u

Exercise 3.8
Fill in the missing letters for the words below.

1.  m__n   5. h__n

2.  r__g   6. f__x

3.  n__t   7. c__n

4.  h__g   8. h__t

Exercise 3.9
Read the sentences and circle the matching pictures.

1. The bug is in the tub.

2. My cat is on the rug.

3. The dog is in the box.

4. The lid is on the pot.

5. Get rid of the fat rat.

6. The pig is in the mud.

7. We had a lot of fun.

Assign the dictations for this lesson
(refer to the instructions).

Also, have your student play the "Short Vowel Rocket
Game" to practice identifying short vowel sounds.
You should also continue to play the "Blast Off Matching
Game" and the "Save the Earth Game" for
this and the previous lesson.

Consonant Blends

1) Review the flash cards.

2) Check the dictations from the previous lesson.

3) If needed, do a warm-up for the CVC combinations (as done in the last lesson) using letter tiles, magnetic letters or a moveable alphabet on a device.
Always use **lowercase** letters.

Consonant blends are when two or three consonants are next to each other and you hear all the sounds of each letter *blended* together.

 ## Read the words below - Beginning Blends.

stop	snag	trap	clot	blot
flit	scab	flat	spat	grub
drat	swim	glad	twin	cram

| | strap | scrap | split | |

 ## Read the words below - Ending Blends.

fast	held	milk	film	mask
lump	left	silk	help	risk
gasp	wilt	self	went	kept

Exercise 4.1
Review: Fill in the blanks to complete the words.

1. p __ __

2. c __ __

3. b __ __

4. f __ __

Exercise 4.2
Write the consonant blends for the <u>beginning</u> sounds for the pictures below.

1. s t ___ ___

2. ___ ___

3. ___ ___

4. ___ ___

5. ___ ___

6. ___ ___

7. ___ ___ ___

8. ___ ___

9. ___ ___

10. ___ ___

Exercise 4.3
Write the consonant blends for the <u>ending</u> sounds for the pictures below.

1.  stu __ __

5. pla __ __

2. te __ __

6. hu __ __

3. li __ __

7. mi __ __

4. la __ __

8. be __ __

Exercise 4.4
Circle the letters that make real words (there is one per line).

1. tw _?_	ig	an	on
2. sw _?_	ut	id	im
3. pl _?_	ug	at	in
4. tr _?_	in	ip	ut
5. gr _?_	in	at	ib

When 'a' sounds like short 'o'

Sometimes 'a' sounds like a short 'o'.
Read the words below,
but use a short 'o' instead of a short 'a'.

b<u>a</u>ld	s<u>a</u>lt	c<u>a</u>lm	w<u>a</u>nt
h<u>a</u>lt	sw<u>a</u>p	p<u>a</u>lm	f<u>a</u>lse

There are many words where 'a' sounds like a short 'o', as well as 'al' as /ul/ (such as "loyal"). Point this out to your student as you see them.

Exercise 4.5

Circle the words that make sense in the sentences.

1. Put the list on my desk / milk.

2. You must ask for held / help when you go.

3. I have a lot of milk in my salt / cup.

4. If you want to go, you must ask / last .

5. The twin can swim calm / fast.

6. He went / held on to the flag.

Consonant Blends in Isolation

See which blends your student can read. These will be on the flash cards and should be reviewed until mastered.

Note that blends can also be in the middle of longer words.

Also, note that very often students confuse 'tr' as 'chr' and 'dr' as 'jr'. These will be addressed in later lessons.

Beginning Blends:

st	br	sn	cl	tr	bl	cr
fl	gr	sc	sp	sm	sl	pl
dr	pr	sw	tw	gl	fr	sk
		str	scr	spl		

Ending Blends:

st	mp	sp	sm	ld	ft	lt
lk	lf	lm	lp	nt	pt	sk

Assign the dictations for this lesson, and have your student play the on-line games for review.

1) Review the flash cards.

2) Check the dictations from the previous lesson.

Often, a group or pair of letters make certain sounds when together.

chop   champ   chip   chap

Words Ending With 'ch'

Words ending with 'ch' usually end with a 'tch'.

atch

etch

itch

otch

utch

all vowels are short

hatch

hitch

blotch

fetch

stitch

A *silent* 't' is *usually* added between the short vowel and the 'ch'.

Note that You do **not** hear the 't', however, you **must** remember it, when spelling.

If a short vowel sound is misidentified, show the flash card and say the name of the image that goes with the vowel.

These words do **not** get the added 't':

rich   su<u>ch</u>   mu<u>ch</u>

And this word has a confused 'a':

short 'o'

w<u>a</u>tch

Exercise 5.1
Circle the sound that completes the word.

1.

h___?____   atch   etch   itch   otch   utch

2.

cr___?____   atch   etch   itch   otch   utch

3.

sw___?____   atch   etch   itch   otch   utch

4.

l___?____   atch   etch   itch   otch   utch

5.

scr___?____   atch   etch   itch   otch   utch

Exercise 5.2
Complete the words below.

1. ch_____ _____

2. ch_____ _____

3. ch_____ _____ _____

4. ri_____ _____

5. _____ _____ itch

6. p_____ _____ _____ _____

Exercise 5.3
Circle the sound to make a real word.

1. sk __?__   itch   etch

2. b __?__   atch   etch

3. cl __?__   itch   utch

4. n __?__   utch   otch

5. sn __?__   atch   utch

6. f __?__   utch   etch

sh   <u>sh</u>op   <u>sh</u>ip   <u>sh</u>ut   <u>sh</u>ot

ash
esh
ish
osh
ush

all
vowels
are
short

r<u>ash</u>

fr<u>esh</u>

f<u>ish</u>

g<u>osh</u>

bl<u>ush</u>

short 'o'

w<u>a</u>sh

 Read the words below.

hutch	sham	latch	trash
patch	shin	chat	smash
clutch	shrug	such	brush
pitch	splash	much	wish

w<u>a</u>sh   w<u>a</u>tch   w<u>a</u>nt

pets - pest   fats - fast

lots - lost   nets - nest

past - pats   spit - pits

Exercise 5.4
Circle the sounds to make real words (there is only one per line).

1. l _?_   osh   ash   itch

2. cr _?_   ash   itch   ish

3. br _?_   etch   ish   ush

4. st _?_   otch   ush   ash

5. h _?_   esh   ush   etch

Exercise 5.5
Choose 'ch' or 'sh' to make real words.

ch   sh

1. cra_____   4. ca_____   7. _____amp

2. _____ut   5. ra_____   8. ba_____

3. _____at   6. pun_____   9. su_____

Assign the dictations for this lesson,
and have your student play the on-line games for review.

The /th/ Sound

'th' makes the two sounds:

1. 'th' makes an airy sound as in "thin".
2. 'th' makes a buzzing sound as in "that".

th   <u>th</u>in   <u>th</u>at   ma<u>th</u>   pa<u>th</u>

 ## Read the words below.

bath	chat	crash	shut	she
this	chop	rich	scratch	me
than	match	such	rash	be
with	trash	much	we	he

w<u>a</u>sh   s<u>a</u>lt

h<u>a</u>lt   sw<u>a</u>p

c<u>a</u>lm   w<u>a</u>nt

w<u>a</u>tch   sw<u>a</u>b

Exercise 6.1

Read the sentences to your student and have him/her complete the words with the sounds listed.

> ash   atch   ush   ish   ath   itch

1. Make a __w_____ on a shooting star.

2. Another name for a tattletale is __sn_____ .

3. If your skin is red and itchy, you may have a

   __r_____ .

4. If you go for a walk in the woods, it is best to stay on the

   __p_____ .

5. The dog tried to __sn_____ the bacon from the table.

6. You can __fl_____ a toilet.

Exercise 6.2

Circle a sound to make a real word (there is one per line).

1. pa_?_	th	sh	ch
2. fl_?_	itch	ash	ish
3. sl_?_	otch	ish	ash
4. ch_?_	on	an	in
5. th_?_	am	in	ish

Exercise 6.3
Complete the words below.

1. l__ __ __

2. p__ __ __ __

3. m__ __ __

4. sw__ __ __ __

5.  p__ __ __

6. f__ __ __

7. b__ __ __

8. br __ __ __

9. m__ __ __ __

10.  cr__ __ __

Exercise 6.4
Read the sentences and circle the words that make sense.

1. Of / He has a pet cat.

2. The man sat on top was / of the box.

3. He / The trap had a latch on the top.

4. My / Me leg had a cramp.

5. Of / Was it hot at camp?

6. Do he / you have a pet fish?

Exercise 6.5
Read each sentence to your student, and have him/her write the missing word.

1. A bird lays eggs in a ____ ____ ____ ____.

2. The opposite of fat is ____ ____ ____ ____.

3. If you don't know where you are, you are

    ____ ____ ____ ____.

4. When you add and subtract, you are doing

    ____ ____ ____ ____.

5. When you blow out birthday candles, you make a

    ____ ____ ____ ____.

6. If you are dirty, you should take a ____ ____ ____ ____.

Exercise 6.6
Circle a sound to make a real word.

1.	bla_?_	th	sh	st
2.	_?_ap	sh	th	sl
3.	fa_?_	st	sh	mp
4.	_?_ip	th	tr	st
5.	_?_at	sh	th	tr

Assign the dictations for this lesson,
and have your student play the on-line games for review.

The /nk/ Sounds

1) Review the flash cards.

2) Check the dictations from the previous lesson.

Normally, 'n' makes the /n/ sound as in "nest".
However, the 'n' in 'nk' makes a different sound.
It makes the sound /nk/ as in "sank".

nk

ank

enk

ink

onk

unk

*The 'a' in 'ank' is long
as in the word "bank",
all other vowels are short.

t<u>ank</u>

st<u>ink</u>

b<u>onk</u>

tr<u>unk</u>

Read the words below.

thank	think	honk	shrink
blank	blink	trunk	scratch
crank	wink	junk	switch
sank	sink	dunk	pitch

Read the following sentences:

1. I think he went to the bank.

2. I do not want to flunk the test.

3. Where did he put the junk?

4. The skunk ran on the path.

5. He has to thank you.

6. The cloth shrank in the wash.

sk<u>unk</u>

Spelling Tip

There are no words that contain the consonant blend 'jr'.
If a word starts with a /jr/ sound, it is *probably* a 'dr'.

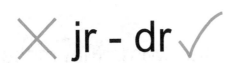 ✗ jr - dr ✓    <u>dr</u>ink

---

Exercise 7.1

Circle the sounds to make real words (there is one per line).

1. dr _?_   ig   ash   ip

2. dr _?_   ank   onk   ish

3. dr _?_   ash   ig   op

4. dr _?_   in   ag   itch

5. dr _?_   am   ink   og

Exercise 7.2
Read the words and circle the answers to the question:

Is the vowel sound in the word **long** or **short**?

1.	n<u>e</u>st	long	short
2.	m<u>e</u>	long	short
3.	l<u>a</u>tch	long	short
4.	b<u>a</u>nk	long	short
5.	w<u>e</u>	long	short
6.	b<u>e</u>	long	short

Exercise 7.3
Read each sentence and circle the words that make sense.

1. She <u>have / has</u> to thank you.

2. He <u>does / was</u> not want to crash the bus.

3. We <u>have / has</u> to go to the bank to get cash.

4. I can not think <u>of / is</u> what to do next.

5. What <u>do / does</u> you think of the pet frog?

Exercise 7.4
Circle the sounds to make real words.

1. p_?___   ank / ink

2. pl_?___   ank / ink

3. cr_?___   ank / ink

4. y_?___   ank / ink

5. l_?___   ank / ink

6. r_?___   unk / ash

7. ch_?___   unk / ash

8. spl_?___   unk / ash

9. cr_?___   unk / ash

10. j_?___   unk / ash

Exercise 7.5
Fill in the 'nk' sounds to complete the words below.

1.   t___ ___ ___

2.   p___ ___ ___

3.   dr___ ___ ___

4.   s___ ___ ___

5.   tr___ ___ ___

6.    b___ ___ ___

Assign the dictations for this lesson, and have your student play the "nk, ck, ng Phonics Game" to practice identifying the 'nk' sounds.

ing

ang

1) Review the flash cards.
2) Check the dictations from the previous lesson.

Normally, 'n' makes the /n/ sound as in "nest".
However, the 'n' in 'ng' makes a different sound.
It makes the sound /ng/ as in "sang".

ang

eng

ing

ong

ung

*The 'a' in 'ang' is long
as in the word "bang",
all other vowels are short.

r<u>ang</u>

l<u>eng</u>th

s<u>ing</u>

l<u>ong</u>

l<u>ung</u>

 Read the words below.

sang	sting	song	think	trunk
hang	ring	strong	stink	dunk
length	wing	clung	blink	match
strength	thing	hung	brink	crash

Read the following sentences:

1. Is the trip long?
2. I think she is wrong.
3. She will sing the song.
4. The cat has the string.
5. The strong man will lift me up.

Exercise 8.1
Circle the words that have the /z/ sound (hint, there are 4).

the   his   of   is   this

was   my   he   do   has

Exercise 8.2
Read the sentences to your student saying "blank" for the incomplete words. Then have him/her complete the words using the listed sounds.

These sounds may be used more than once or not at all

ank   enk   ink   onk   unk

1. It is polite to say "please" and " th_____ you".

2. The truck will h_____ its horn.

3. The twins slept in b_____ beds.

4. The mouse ate a ch_____ of cheese.

5. The girl went to the ice-skating r_____.

Exercise 8.3
Circle the sounds to make real words.

1. cr __?__   ank / ang

2. bl __?__   unk / ink

3. str __?__   ong / onk

4. str __?__   ink / ing

5. ch __?__   unk / ong

6. cl __?__   ung / ong

Exercise 8.4
Read the sentences to your student saying "blank" for the incomplete words. Then have him/her complete the words using the listed sounds.

These sounds may be used more than once or not at all

ang   eng   ing   ong   ung

1. The bird will __s_____ in the morning.

2. The opposite of short is __l_____.

3. The man sang a __s_____.

4. The lady had a __r_____ on her finger.

5. The bee __st_____ my leg.

6. The bat will __h_____ upside down to sleep.

Exercise 8.5
Complete the words below.

1. w___ ___ ___

2. k___ ___ ___

3. l___ ___ ___

4. t___ ___ ___

5. str___ ___ ___

6.  s___ ___ ___

7. tr___ ___ ___

8. dr___ ___ ___

9. r___ ___ ___

10. s___ ___ ___

11. w___ ___ ___

12. sk___ ___ ___

Assign the dictations for this lesson, and have your student play the "nk, ck, ng Phonics Game" to practice identifying the 'ng' & 'nk' sounds.

ing

ang

1) Review the flash cards.
2) Check the dictations from the previous lesson.

This lesson introduces the 'ck' sound. Note that students often confuse 'ck' and 'nk' sounds. If this happens, point out the differences and give a lot of practice.

ck

ack

eck

ick

ock

uck

*All vowels are short.

stack   block

speck   stuck

brick

brick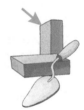

 Read the words below.

black	tuck	pocket	wink
back	truck	rocket	tank
clock	sack	ticket	trunk
lock	slack	picket	sprung

Read the following sentences:

1. Stack the bricks in the back of the shelf.
2. He stuck the stick into the mud.
3. Wish me luck on my math test.
4. The duck was on the raft.
5. The dog will fetch the stick.
6. He will lock the box with the latch.

Exercise 9.1

Read each sentence to your student, and have him/her complete the sentences with the words that make sense.

stuck	stack	luck
back	trick	brick

1. He played a _____ on me!

2. People think a rabbit's foot is good _____.

3. The sign said that he will be _____ soon.

4. The truck got _____ in the mud.

5. The strong house was made of _____.

6. The boy ate a _____ of pancakes.

Exercise 9.2

Read the words to your student and have him/her circle the correct beginning sounds.

1. __?__ust   tr   chr   5. __?__ip   chr   tr

2. __?__ink   jr   dr   6. __?__op   dr   jr

3. __?__ip   jr   dr   7. __?__ap   chr   tr

4. __?__ag   jr   dr   8. __?__ank   dr   jr

Exercise 9.3

Fill in the 'ck' sounds to complete the words.

1. s __ __ __

2. sn__ __ __

3. s__ __ __

4. r__ __ __

5. d__ __ __

6. tr__ __ __

7. cl__ __ __

8. bl__ __ __

9. t__ __ __

10. k__ __ __

Exercise 9.4
Circle the sounds that make real words.

1. p____ ?____   ack   etch
5. tr____ ?____   uck   atch

2. sw____ ?____   etch   itch
6. dr____ ?____   ink   ick

3. sn____ ?____   ick   ack
7. tr____ ?____   ink   ick

4. sn____ ?____   uck   ock
8. st____ ?____   onk   ick

Exercise 9.5
Complete the sentences with the words that make sense.

to   the   have   is

1. The duck _____ in the pond.

2. The truck got stuck in _____ mud.

3. He has _____ go back to the bank.

4. I _____ a lot of luck.

Assign the dictations for this lesson, and have your student play the "nk, ck, ng Phonics Game" to practice identifying the 'ng', 'nk' & 'ck' sounds.

1) Review the flash cards.
2) Check the dictations from the previous lesson.

'ay' *always* makes the long 'a' sound.

ay

d<u>ay</u>   w<u>ay</u>   pl<u>ay</u>

tod<u>ay</u>   sw<u>ay</u>   aw<u>ay</u>*

* The first 'a' in "away" sounds like a short 'o'.

In a *few* words, 'ey' also makes the long 'a' sound.

ey

gr<u>ey</u>   pr<u>ey</u>   conv<u>ey</u>   surv<u>ey</u>*

th<u>ey</u>   h<u>ey</u>   ob<u>ey</u>*

*Sounds in these words have not yet been covered.

Read the words below.

may	itch	plum	pluck
spray	snitch	such	black
stay	hitch	much	lick
clay	hatch	rich	tuck
bank	pink	sung	speck
tank	stink	lung	track
drank	blink	hung	pick

Exercise 10.1
Read the sentences and circle the words that make sense.

1. They will be _stung / back_ at sunset.

2. He must _stay / hung_ and play with his dog.

3. I have to _play / check_ in on my pets.

4. They have to _pack / spray_ for the trip.

5. What is the _way / patch_ to get back to the camp?

6. She _sway / may_ not want to stop and rest.

Exercise 10.2
Fill in the missing sounds to complete the words.

1. pr__ __

6. s__ __ __

2. t__ __ __

7. l__ __ __

3. tr__ __

8. w__ __ __

4. r__ __ __

9. d__ __ __

5. cr__ __ __ __

10. tr__ __ __

Exercise 10.3
Circle the sounds to make real words (there is one per line).

1. pr __?__   ath   ank   ack

2. pl __?__   ay   ick   ath

3. shr __?__   ath   ank   ack

4. str __?__   ank   ack   ong

5. st __?__   ong   onk   ick

Exercise 10.4
Read the sentences to your student, saying "blank" for the word in question. Have your student circle the word that makes sense.

1. The dog had no owners, he was a spray / stray.

2. During the storm, the trees sway / play in the wind.

3. The cat likes to pray / play with the string.

4. The bowl was made of bay / clay.

5. They told us to stay / sway until the show was over.

6. The opposite of night is day / may.

7. We will play / pay the waiter for our meal.

Exercise 10.5
Read the clues to your student and have him/her complete the puzzle.

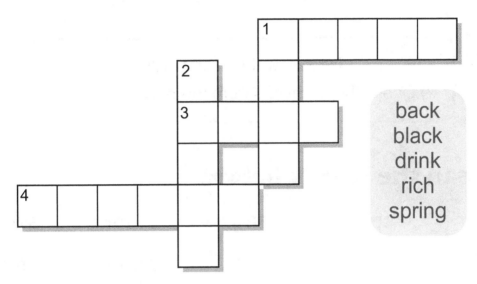

back
black
drink
rich
spring

Across

1. The opposite of white is ___ .

3. The opposite of poor is ___ .

4. The season before summer is ___ .

Down

1. The opposite of front is ___ .

2. Something you do with juice___ .

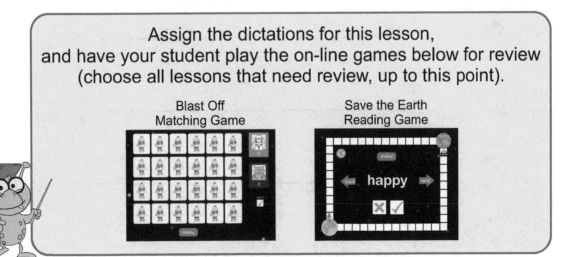

Assign the dictations for this lesson,
and have your student play the on-line games below for review
(choose all lessons that need review, up to this point).

Blast Off
Matching Game

Save the Earth
Reading Game

Review: Lessons 1-10

1) Review the flash cards.
2) Check the dictations from the previous lesson.

 Read the words below.

red	spit	hang	chunk	switch
sad	from	thing	hung	tray
man	stink	truck	lung	trash
bed	bring	blink	hitch	patch

Exercise R1.1

Write the words for each of the pictures below.

  1._____

  2._____

  3._____

  4._____

  5._____

Exercise R1.2
Fill in the missing letters for the word below.

1.  br___ ___ ___

2. cl___ ___ ___

3. t___ ___ ___

4. tr___ ___ ___

5. c___ ___ ___ ___

6. br___ ___ ___

Exercise R1.3
Draw lines to match the words to their pictures.

1. trunk

2. lung

3. sing

4. skunk

5. sink

6. strong

7. drink

8. honk

Exercise R1.4

Read the clues to your student and have him/her write the words, using the clues, on the lines.

1. Change the underlined letter in the word so it becomes something in your body that helps you breathe.

   <u>h</u>ung _____

2. Change the underlined letters so the word becomes another word for "garbage".

   <u>sm</u>ash _____

3. Change the underlined letters, so the word becomes what your brain does.

   <u>bl</u>ink _____

4. Change the underlined letter so the word means opposite of front.

   <u>h</u>ack _____

5. Change the underlined letters to make the word mean opposite of "go".

   <u>dr</u>op _____

Exercise R1.5

Read the clues to your student, and have him/her complete the puzzle.

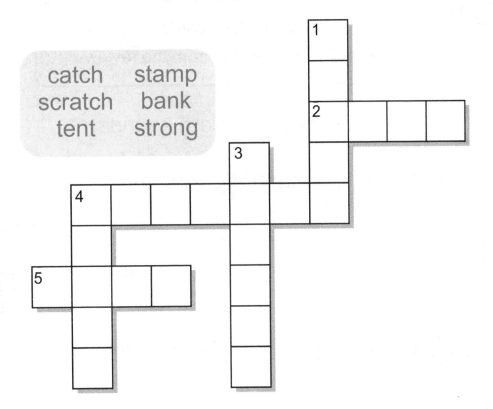

catch   stamp
scratch   bank
tent   strong

Down

1. You use a baseball mitt to __ a ball.

3. The opposite of weak, is __.

4. To send a letter you need a __.

Across

2. When you go camping, you pitch a __.

4. You __ an itch.

5. You put money in a __.

Review all lessons up to this point using the on-line games.

The /oo/ Sounds

'oo' has <u>three</u> different sounds.

The 1st 'oo' sound: "long" /oo/ as in "boo".

1

cool   root   hoop   tooth

Boo!

The 2nd 'oo' sound: "short" /oo/ as in "good".

2

hood   hook   foot   look

The 3rd 'oo' sound: a short 'u' sound.

3

blood   flood

Note that the word "long" is not to be confused with "long vowels". In long 'oo' words, the sound can last a long time in comparison to the short 'oo' words, where the 'oo' sound comes quick and is in shorter duration.

Read the words below.

booth	spoon	fool	hoop	long
broom	room	pool	loop	'oo'
soon	tool	cool	boot	

wood	took	book	cook	short
good	shook	brook	look	'oo'

Read the words below.

shot - shoot   drop - droop

rot - root   cop - coop

hot - hoot   hop - hoop

lot - loot   stop - stoop

'ou' as /oo/

'ou' sometimes has the /oo/ as in "boo" sound.

group   soup   wound   through

soup = /soop/

Exercise 11.1
Draw lines to match the rhyming words.

1. bloom   shook

2. group   good

3. flood   gloom

4. took   blood

5. stood   hoop

Exercise 11.2
Complete the sentences with the words that make sense.

food	black	foot
play	hook	frog

1. The witch had a _____ hat.

2. I put the boot on my _____ .

3. The cat will _____ with the string.

4. A _____ may jump into the pool.

5. Put the bags of _____ in the trunk.

6. Hang the hat on the _____ .

Exercise 11.3

Read the following sentences to your student and then have him/her circle the words that make sense.

1. The opposite of "bad" is wood / good.

2. The fish was caught on a hook / book.

3. The past tense of "shake" is shook / shoot.

4. The past tense of "take" is toot / took.

5. Something we do with our eyes is book / look.

Exercise 11.4

Read the following sentences to your student and then have him/her complete the sentences with the words that make sense.

broom	bedroom	bloom
soon	noon	moon

1. The cow jumped over the _____.

2. People eat lunch at _____.

3. All my stuff is in my _____.

4. We sweep the floor with a _____.

5. In the spring, flowers will _____.

6. _____ means "at any moment now".

Exercise 11.5
Complete the words below.

1. m__ __ __

2. sp__ __ __

3. br__ __ __

4. f__ __ __

5. h__ __ __

6. b__ __ __

Exercise 11.6
Read each sentence and circle the words that make sense.

1. He swept the room with a boom / broom.

2. She put the book on the plant / shelf.

3. He got mad and took / shook his fist at me.

4. It took a long / good time to get to the bank.

5. She drank the broth with a soon / spoon.

6. Do not look into the sun / moon.

Assign the dictations for this lesson,
and have your student play the on-line games for review.

> 1) Review the flash cards.
> 2) Check the dictations from the previous lesson.

'qu' makes the /kw/ sound
as in "quit".

qu   quit   quack   quick   quest

 ## Read the words below.

quit	loot	book	foot
quack	zoo	took	boot
quick	zoom	quiz	flung
quilt	luck	help	lung

broom	stay	clock
doom	play	track
balloon	clay	stack

Read the following sentences:

1. Do not quit the play.

2. He took a quiz at school.

3. He was quick to run away.

4. She took the quilt to bed.

5. He went on a quest.

Exercise 12.1
Circle the sounds to make real words (there is one per line).

1. qu_?_	ing	ick	ink
2. st_?_	eck	ay	ush
3. shr_?_	atch	ish	ank
4. th_?_	otch	ish	ink
5. qu_?_	est	an	ing

Exercise 12.2
Read each sentence and complete the missing words with the correct sounds.

ay   oo   ick

1. The dog ran ___aw_____.

2. The cat will ___pl_____ with the string.

3. The dog will do a ___tr_____.

4. I wish I had a ___g_____d___ book.

5. He swept the room with a ___br_____m__.

6. You must be ___qu_____ to catch the rat!

Exercise 12.3

Read the clues to your student and have him/her write the new words on the lines.

1. Change the underlined letters in the word so that it becomes another word for "fast".

   trick _____

2. Change underlined letters in the word so it becomes something a duck says.

   track _____

3. Change the word so that it becomes the name of the utensil that you use to eat ice-cream and soup.

   moon _____

4. Change the word so it becomes something that you use to sweep with.

   room _____

5. Change the underlined letter in the word so it becomes something you eat.

   mood _____

6. Change the underlined letters in the word so it becomes the word for when you want to stop doing something.

   quiz _____

Exercise 12.4

Read the sentences and circle the matching pictures.

1. They say this brings good luck.

2. He is looking at his book.

3. He sat at a desk and took a quiz.

4. The cat was quick to catch the rat.

5. He hung his hat on the hook.

6. Put the quilt on the bed.

Assign the dictations for this lesson,
and have your student play the on-line games below for this
lesson as well as prior lessons that need review.

Blast Off
Matching Game

Save the Earth
Reading Game

The /nch/ Sounds

nch

anch

ench

inch

onch

unch

* All vowels are short.

ranch   conch

bench   hunch

pinch

 lunch

 ## Read the words below.

branch	stink	hang	clutch
quench	stunk	fling	catch
wrench	stung	stench	scratch
crunch	sting	bench	clench

rack	stack	black	crack
rank	stank	blank	crank

Exercise 13.1
Complete the words below with the 'nch' sounds.

1. wr__ __ __ __

2. p__ __ __ __

3. b__ __ __ __

4.  br__ __ __ __

5. l__ __ __ __

6. __ __ __ __

Exercise 13.2
Read the sentences to your student and have him/her complete the words with the sounds listed.

> ick   ank   oo   uck   anch   inch   ack

1. We saw a chimp at the z_____ .

2. My grandmother likes to p_____ my cheeks.

3. The birds were perched on a br_____ .

4. If you eat too much, you may get s_____ .

5. There was a cr_____ in the sidewalk.

6. Our car got st_____ in the snow.

7. Fill in the bl_____ to answer the question.

Exercise 13.3
Read the sentences and complete the words.

uck   ong   atch   etch   ank   ack

1. The chick will soon h__ __ __ __ .

2. On the trip, I want to sit in the b__ __ __ of the van.

3. Wish me good l__ __ __ on my test.

4. My dog will play f__ __ __ __ with me.

5. My pants shr__ __ __ in the wash.

6. The str__ __ __ man will lift the box.

Exercise 13.4
Circle the sounds to make real words (there is one per line).

1. p_?_	unch	anch	ench
2. p_?_	onch	ench	inch
3. br_?_	inch	anch	onch
4. st_?_	otch	itch	atch
5. bl_?_	ick	uck	ack
6. sw_?_	oo	ay	ick

Exercise 13.5

Read the following clues to your student, and have him/her write the new words on the lines provided.

1. Change the underlined letter to finish the sentence: A magician does a magic ___.

   tr<u>u</u>ck _____

2. Change the underlined letter in the word to make it something you sit on in a park.

   b<u>u</u>nch _____

3. Change the underlined letter in the word to make it something that you find in a library.

   <u>t</u>ook _____

4. Change the underlined letter in the word to make it something someone does when they tightly squeeze your skin with their fingers.

   p<u>u</u>nch _____

5. Change the underlined letter in the word so it becomes the opposite of bad.

   <u>h</u>ood _____

Assign the dictations for this lesson, and have your student play the on-line games for review.

1) Review the flash cards.
2) Check the dictations from the previous lesson.

In many words, 'y' at the end
of a word sounds like a long 'i'.

y

| fl<u>y</u> | fr<u>y</u> | tr<u>y</u> | sp<u>y</u> |
| b<u>y</u> | cr<u>y</u> | m<u>y</u> | dr<u>y</u> |

'igh' can also make the long 'i' sound.

igh

s<u>igh</u>   th<u>igh</u>   n<u>igh</u>t   br<u>igh</u>t

Read the words below.

shy	high	pool	took	crunch
pry	sight	hoop	book	branch
sky	fight	broom	foot	quit
why	tight	shoot	look	quilt

| puck | truck | duck | tack | sack |
| punk | trunk | dunk | tank | sank |

Exercise 14.1
Read each sentence to your student, using the word "blank" for the missing words. Have him/her complete the sentences with the words below.

fly	why	cry	night
shy	try	by	right

1. He will ___try___ to jump over the puddle.

2. We go to bed at _____.

3. The baby will _____ when he's hungry.

4. The little boy was very _____ around new people.

5. The opposite of left is _____.

6. The story was written _____ a little girl.

7. _____ did the girl have to leave early?

8. This summer, we will _____ on an airplane.

Exercise 14.2
Circle a sound to make a real word.

1. th_?_   onk   (ink)   4. sh_?_   igh   (y)
2. th_?_   (igh) ath   5. sh_?_   (ack) ath
3. th_?_   ack   (ing)   6. sh_?_   unk   (ock)

Exercise 14.3
Read the clues to your student and have him/her circle the answer.

1. The opposite of low is: <u>high / shy</u>

2. The opposite of day is: <u>sky / night</u>

4. The opposite of wet is: <u>dry / fry</u>

5. The opposite of dim is: <u>sight / bright</u>

6. The opposite of wrong is: <u>fight / right</u>

Exercise 14.4
Read the sentences and choose the correct sounds to complete the missing words.

uck	ock	ick	unk	ank

1. The fish swam in the __t_____ .

2. My foot got __st_____ in the mud.

3. The twins had __b_____ beds.

4. I put my foot in the __s_____ .

5. The dog will fetch the __st_____ .

Exercise 14.5
Draw lines to match the words to their pictures.

1. thigh

2. sunlight

3. fight

4. spy

5. night

6. cry

7. fly

8. fry

Assign the dictations for this lesson,
and have your student play the on-line games for review.

1) Review the flash cards.
2) Check the dictations from the previous lesson.

Both 'oy and 'oi' have the same sound.

oy   b<u>oy</u>   t<u>oy</u>   s<u>oy</u>   pl<u>oy</u>

'oy' is usually at the **end** of a word.

oi   b<u>oi</u>l   s<u>oi</u>l   f<u>oi</u>l   c<u>oi</u>l

'oi' is usually in the **middle** of a word.

Read the words below.

toy	annoy	coin	light
joy	alloy	boil	flight
boy	void	join	dry
ploy	avoid*	oil	spy
soy	point	broil	pinch
royal*	joint	hoist	spoon

* The 'a' in "royal" and "avoid" sounds like a /uh/.

Read the following:

1. The soil in the box is moist.
2. The tinfoil is on the shelf.
3. The coil got hot.
4. He will broil the fish.
5. Point at the boy in your class.

Exercise 15.1

Read the sentences and complete the missing words using a sound listed. Note that the sounds in the box may be used more than once or not at all.

| ank | igh | inch | ench | oy | oi | oo |

1. Bring the soup to a b__ __ l.

2. I sat on the b__ __ __ __ to rest.

3. Wrap the sandwich in tinf__ __l.

4. The b__ __s will play in the back of the room.

5. Put the plant into the s__ __l.

6. We dr__ __ __ milk with the snack.

7. A wrench is a t__ __l.

8. He kept his t__ __s in the red box.

Exercise 15.2
Complete the words below.

1. c _ _ _

2. sw_ _ _ _

3.  t_ _ box

4. b_ _ _

5. p_ _ _ _ _

6. p_ _ _ _

7. dr_ _ _ _

8. c_ _ _ _

Exercise 15.3
Circle the words that make the most sense.

1. He will try to catch a _fish / lamp_ with his net.

2. He wants to scoop the sand into the _bucket / pool_ .

3. He will _join / broil_ the fish for lunch.

4. She put the quilt on the _bed / skunk_.

5. She will toss the _coin / kitten_ into the well.

6. He wants to shoot _chimps / hoops_ today.

7. We went for a swim in the _drool / pool_ .

Exercise 15.4

Read the following clues to your student, and have him/her write the new words on the lines provided.

1. Change the underlined letter so the word becomes the opposite of "loose".

 <u>n</u>ight _____

2. Change the underlined letter in the word to make it something that water does when it gets very hot.

 <u>c</u>oil _____

3. Change the underlined letter in the word to make it another word that means "happy".

 <u>b</u>oy _____

4. Change the underlined letter so the word becomes one that describes a hammer or screw driver.

 <u>f</u>ool _____

5. Change the underlined letter in the word so it becomes the singular word for "teeth".

 <u>b</u>ooth _____

Assign the dictations for this lesson,
and have your student play the on-line games for review.

1) Review the flash cards.
2) Check the dictations from the previous lesson.

When a vowel comes before
the letter 'r', it has a special sound.

ar   er   ir   or   ur

c<u>ar</u>   h<u>er</u>   b<u>ir</u>d   ch<u>or</u>e   c<u>ur</u>b

'er' , 'ir' and 'ur' all have the **same** sound.

ar

'ar' sounds like 'r'.
Think of what a pirate says.
He says, "Arrrrr!"

Arrrr!

or

'or' itself is a word as in "this *or* that".
It is also found in many other words.
*Note: in words that **end** with the /or/ sound
there is often a "do nothing" 'e' at the end.*

Read the words below.

| cart | yard | part | farm |
| start | hard | smart | alarm |

| for | torn | cork | befor<u>e</u> |
| form | born | sport | wor<u>e</u> |

Exercise 16.1
Complete the words below (each word has the /ar/ sound).

1. st __ __

2. c __ __

3. b __ __ __

4. j __ __

5. sh __ __ __

6. ch __ __ __

7. c __ __ __ s

8. __ __ __

Exercise 16.2
Complete the words below (each word has the /or/ sound).

Remember, many words that end with the /or/ sound have a "do nothing" 'e' at the end.

1. c __ __ __

2. st __ __ __

3. c __ __ __

4. th __ __ __

5. sn __ __ __

6. h __ __ __ e

7. h __ __ __

8. sc __ __ __

'er', 'ir' and 'ur' all have the *same* sound.

st<u>er</u>n   b<u>ir</u>d   b<u>ur</u>n

Exercise 16.3
Draw lines to match the words with their pictures.

1. th<u>ir</u>d

2. ch<u>ur</u>ch

3. sk<u>ir</u>t

4. f<u>ir</u>st

5. sh<u>ir</u>t

3rd

6. s<u>ur</u>f

7. b<u>ir</u>d

1st

8. t<u>ur</u>n

Exercise 16.4
Read the sentences and circle the words that make sense.

1. Her car is not far from the <u>snore / store</u>.

2. He has a black <u>marker / core</u> in his box.

3. They have no <u>more / dark</u> snacks on the shelf.

4. She wore a pink skirt to <u>church / porch</u>.

5. The smart boy will <u>curl / turn</u> the light on.

6. He got a sunburn at the <u>market / shore</u>.

7. Turn the car so you do not hit the <u>curb / charm</u>.

Exercise 16.5
The words below have **extra letters** that are not needed.
Each word has the /or/ sound. Cross out the unused letters.

door   floor   poor   your   four

The sentences below have words that do not sound the way that they are spelled. These words are in **bold.**
Read the sentences out loud.

1. I do not have to **work** on Sunday.

2. The **worm** is under the dirt.

3. I will **warn** him not to go to **war**.

4. It was a **warm** day.

5. Lots of **words** are in a book.

we̲r̲e̲

we̲r̲e̲: This is the /w/ sound and the /er/ sound with a "do nothing" 'e' at the end.

we̲'r̲e̲: This a contraction for "we are". In a contraction, two words are pushed together, a letter gets popped out, and an apostrophe takes its place.

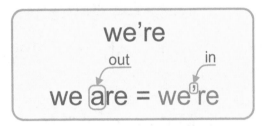

Exercise 16.6

Read the sentences and circle the words that make sense.

1. The stars <u>was / were</u> in the night sky.

2. The night <u>was / were</u> cool.

3. <u>Were / We're</u> going to the park.

4. The girl <u>was / were</u> in her bedroom.

5. The group of kids <u>was / were</u> in the pool.

Assign the dictations for this lesson, and have your student play the on-line "'R' Controlled Vowels Rocket Game".

1) Review the flash cards.
2) Check the dictations from the previous lesson.

Pinch yourself, here come the ouches!!!
There are two ways to get the /ou/ sound as in "ouch".

1

ou

/ou/ as "ouch"

pout   out   shout   loud

2

ow

/ou/ as "ouch"

cow   plow   how   now

'ow' can also sound like a long 'o',
which is found in many words.

long 'o'

ow

crow   bowl   flow   grow

If there's more than one sound for
'ow', how do I know which one to
use when reading?

Try it one way and see if it sounds like a word
you know. Then ask yourself if it makes sense
in the sentence you are reading.

In **_some_** words 'ou' has the /oo/ sound.
Some of these words are listed below:

gr<u>ou</u>p   s<u>ou</u>p   w<u>ou</u>nd   thr<u>ou</u>gh

 ### Read the words below.

cloud	sound	town	slow	snow
snout	ground	frown	bowl	flow
proud	pound	gown	throw	follow

Exercise 17.1

Draw lines to match the pictures to the words.

1. p<u>ow</u>er

2. <u>ow</u>l

3. cl<u>ow</u>n

4. cl<u>ou</u>d

5. sh<u>ou</u>t

6. m<u>ou</u>se

Exercise 17.2
Circle the picture that goes with the word.

1.	bow			
2.	bowl			
3.	blow			
4.	crow			
5.	flower			
6.	shower			
7.	house			
8.	mouth			
9.	cow			

Exercise 17.3
Read the sentences and choose the correct sounds to complete the missing words.

> ay   oo   or   ar   ur   ou   ow

1. His house is not too far from t___ ___ n .

2. After the st___ ___m, we lost our power.

3. Do you think an owl is sm___ ___t ?

4. What was the girl shouting ab___ ___t ?

5. Park the car next to the c___ ___ b .

6. At lunch, they put the food on a tr___ ___ .

7. The loose t___ ___ th is in my mouth.

Exercise 17.4
Circle the sounds that make real words.

1. p__?__l   oo   ou   4. r__?__   ar   ow

2. cl__?__d   oo   ou   5. bl__?__   ar   ow

3. st__?__t   oo   ou   6. f__?__   ar   ow

Exercise 17.5

Circle the words that make sense for each sentence below.

1. The boy will throw the bat on the <u>cloud / ground</u>.

2. How long did the girl sit on the <u>stool / clown</u> ?

3. The drums <u>were / was</u> loud.

4. The girl got lost in the <u>crown / crowd</u> .

5. If you follow the boy you might get <u>lost / snow</u>.

6. My father does not <u>mow / own</u> a red car.

7. In the winter, it might <u>snow / shout</u>.

8. We're about to have our <u>crow / lunch</u>.

9. We found a red dog <u>horse / house</u> for our dog.

10. The boy took a <u>shower / shouting</u> in the morning.

Assign the dictations for this
lesson, and have your student
play the on-line game "ow/ou,
oy/oi, igh, oo, ay Phonics Game".

For Reference

Spelling Hints - 'ou' or 'ow' for /ou/

1. If the /ou/ is at the end of the word, then it is probably '**ow**'.

h<u>ow</u>   c<u>ow</u>   n<u>ow</u>

2. If the /ou/ sound is in the middle of the word, try writing it both ways and see which way looks right. The more you read, the better you'll get.

cl<u>ou</u>n

cl<u>ow</u>n ✓

3. If the word has the /out/ sound, always use 'ou'.

sh<u>out</u>   cl<u>out</u>   ab<u>out</u>   sc<u>out</u>   p<u>out</u>

Below are all of the common words where 'ow' = long 'o'

arrow	elbow	glow	low	shadow	throw
blow	fellow	grow	lower	show	tomorrow
blown	flow	hollow	own	snow	tow
bowl	flown	know	pillow	stow	window
crow	follow	known	row	swallow	yellow

The /ew/ Sound

'ew' usually has the /oo/ sound, as in "boo".

/oo/

ew

grew   drew   flew   brew ─ /oo/

In just a *few* words, 'ew' sounds like 'u'.
These words are listed below.

'u'

ew

few   spew   nephew ─ 'u'

skew   curfew

* 'ph' has /f/ has not yet been taught, however, students often already know this sound.

 ## Read the words below.

chew	blew	jewel	follow	group
crew	few	cashew	flower	soup
new	skew	mildew	shower	spout

| | sound | ground | hound | |
| | found | bound | pound | |

should   would   could

In the words above, the 'ould' makes the same sound as the 'ood' in "good".

Spelling hint: for 'ould' use the following:

"owls use laundry detergent"

Read the words below.

grow	took	could	group
growl	shook	would	soup
coil	look	should	smooth
spoil	brook	good	mouth

Exercise 18.1
For each line, circle the sound that makes a real word.

1. b _?_	orn	ew
2. t _?_	oin	own
3. gr _?_	ore	ew
4. fl _?_	ew	ay
5. scr _?_	ow	ew

Exercise 18.2

Read the sentences to your student and have him/her write the correct words on the lines provided. Not all words in the box below are used.

drew	threw	shower	could
row	bowl	crew	flew

1. I wish I _____ go to the zoo.

2. The baseball player _____ the ball.

3. The birds _____ away.

4. Instead of a bath, I will take a _____.

5. The ship had a _____ of ten sailors.

6. On a cold day, it's nice to have a _____ of soup.

7. The boy _____ pictures with crayons.

Exercise 18.3

Circle the word that is correctly spelled and read it out loud.

1.	tirn / turn		4.	boyl / boil
2.	croud / crowd		5.	houl / howl
3.	bloo / blew		6.	grew / groo

Exercise 18.4
Circle the *three* words that have the **long 'i'** sound.

play	try	right	high
bang	fool	tray	boil

Exercise 18.5
Circle the sounds that match (there is one per line).

1.	er	oo	oy	ir	ow
2.	ew	oo	oy	ir	ow
3.	ou	oo	oy	ir	ow
4.	ur	oo	oy	ir	ow
5.	oi	oo	oy	ir	ow

Exercise 18.6
Circle the *four* words that rhyme with "wood".

food	stood	pool
could	should	tool
droop	cool	hood

Assign the dictations for this lesson,
and have your student play the on-line games for review.

1) Review the flash cards.

2) Check the dictations from the previous lesson.

Before proceeding, tell your student that 'V' stands for "vowel" and 'C' stands for "consonant".

Up to this point, vowels (that are alone) have had **short** vowel sounds. Now, we will see how a vowel can become **long** when another vowel is nearby.

Part 1:

VCV

If just one hop, the first vowel will talk!

The VCV Long Vowel Rule

 hope — When a vowel is one jump to the left of another vowel, it becomes a LONG vowel. Here, 'o' becomes long.

hoping — Note that it can be ANY vowel that makes the first vowel long, not just 'e'. Here, 'o' also becomes long because of the 'i'.

 Usually the 'e' is silent - that's why we sometimes call it "silent 'e'".

 flute

long 'u' *usually* sounds like /oo/, as in "boo".

Read the silent 'e' words below.

tub - t<u>u</u>be	can - c<u>a</u>ne	spin - sp<u>i</u>ne	rat - r<u>a</u>te
rip - r<u>i</u>pe	man - m<u>a</u>ne	fin - f<u>i</u>ne	tot - t<u>o</u>te
cap - c<u>a</u>pe	shin - sh<u>i</u>ne	mad - m<u>a</u>de	hid - h<u>i</u>de

Exercise 19.1
Read the sentences and circle the words that make sense.

1. Tack / Take a look at his new car.

2. Pound the stack / stake into the ground.

3. They want to swim in the lack / lake.

4. He will rake / rack up points in his game.

5. The girl will try to back / bake a cake.

6. After lunch we will have a snake / snack.

Exercise 19.2
Use the **V**CV rule to find the long vowels in the letter groups below. Draw arrows from the second vowel to the first vowel that gets turned long. Underline the long vowel.

1. p<u>o</u>ta

2. stimog

3. amibr

4. opit

5. umotx

6. imat

7. lobut

8. flita

Exercise 19.3

First read the words in the box below, and then complete the sentences with the words that make sense. Not all words are used.

rip	shin	rod	fin	tub	kit
ripe	shine	rode	fine	tube	kite

1. Another word for "good" is _____.

2. When I take a bath, I go into my _____.

3. She _____ a brown horse.

4. At the park, we flew a _____.

5. If your pants are too tight, they may _____.

6. In the morning, the sun will _____.

7. I will make a bird house with a _____.

8. She put the blood into a test- _____.

9. A kick in the _____ can hurt.

10. The man had shark _____ soup.

 It is suggested that you break this lesson into two parts.

Part 2:

The VV Long Vowel Rule

foam

When two vowels are next to each other, the first one usually becomes long and the second one is usually silent. Here, 'o' becomes long and the 'a' is silent.

The Common Vowel Teams

'u' or /oo/

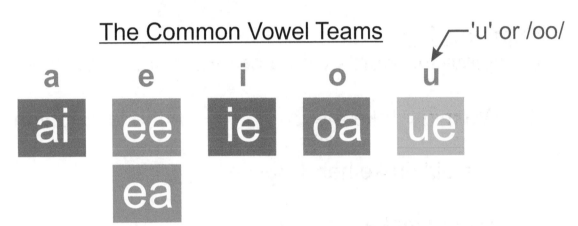

a   e   i   o   u

ai ee ie oa ue

ea

When <u>vowel teams</u> go walking, the **first one** does the talking!

 Read the vowel team words below.

p<u>ai</u>l	b<u>ea</u>t	g<u>oa</u>l
tr<u>ai</u>n	l<u>ea</u>f	r<u>oa</u>st

Remember: long 'u' usually sounds like /oo/ as in "boo"!

t<u>ee</u>th	p<u>ie</u>	gl<u>ue</u>
w<u>ee</u>k	d<u>ie</u>d	bl<u>ue</u>

Exercise 19.4
Fill in the vowel pairs for the **common** long vowel teams.

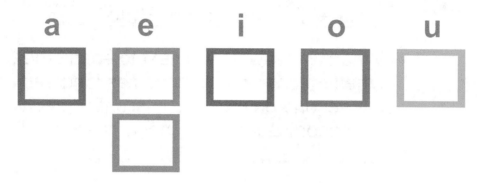

Exercise 19.5
Complete the words with a **common** long vowel team.

1. We might take the b___ ___t on the lake tonight.

2. The girl broke her fingern___ ___l.

3. We will make pumpkin p___ ___.

4. If something is not false then it is tr___ ___.

5. It might r___ ___n later today.

6. The dog always wags his t___ ___l.

7. I like to fl___ ___t on the tube in the pool.

8. I had a p___ ___n in my neck from watching the game.

9. The ink from the pen may st___ ___n your shirt.

10. Our flag is red, white and bl___ ___.

Vowel teams can be **any two vowels** that are together, not just our *common* teams. Note that this does **not** include our special sounds such as 'oi' and 'ou'.

fruit

'ui' is not a common vowel team, but the 'i' still makes the 'u' long (/oo/).

 In vowel teams, the first vowel becomes LONG and the second vowel is *usually* silent, but sometimes it has the **short** vowel sound.

died   diet

Exercise 19.6

Circle the words that make sense in the sentences below.

1. My teacher said to be quite / quiet.

2. My dad wore a blue suit / fruit to work.

3. The lion / line will roar at the crowd.

4. The ink from the pen will ruin / paint your shirt.

5. The poet will read her diet / poem to us.

6. Put the fruit / suit in the basket.

Exercise 19.7
Read the sentences and complete the words with the sounds in the box below.

| ar | ir | oi | ou | ai | ee |

1. The king and qu___ ___n sat on a throne.

2. The dog ran around the y___ ___d.

3. The b___ ___d sat up high on a branch.

4. He broke his finger right on the j___ ___nt.

5. The pig stuck his sn___ ___t into the food bucket.

6. The house needs a new coat of p___ ___nt .

Exercise 19.8
Circle the sounds that make real words. There are two for each line.

1. fl _?___   ow   ou   ew

2. gr _?__   own   oi   ew

3. ch _?__   ore   ew   ir

Assign the dictations for this lesson, and have your student play the on-line game "Long Vowel Rocket Game".

For Reference

ee	
agree	kneel
bee	peek*
beef	queen
beep	reek
between	see
bleed	seed
breeze	seek
cheek	seem*
cheese	seen
creek*	sheep
creep	sheet
deep	sleep
deer*	sneeze
fee	speed
feed	steel*
feel	street
feet	sweet
flee*	teen
free	teeth
freeze	three
greed	tree
greet	tweet
heel*	weed
jeep	week*
keep	weep
knee	wheel

*These words are homophones.
Not all homophones are noted.

ea	
appear	gear
beach	heal*
bead	heat
beam	leader
bean	leaf
beard	leak
beast	lean
beat	leap
bleach	leash
bleak	mean
breathe	meat*
cheap	near
cheat	neat
clean	peach
clear	peak*
creak*	peanut
cream	please
crease	preach
deal	reach
dear*	rear
dream	scream
each	seat
eagle	seam*
ear	steal*
east	steam
easy	stream
fear	teach
flea*	treat
freak	weak*

Adding the Suffix 'ing'

1) Review the flash cards.

2) Check the dictations from the previous lesson.

Before proceeding, you may want to tell your student what a "suffix" is.

There are two rules you must know to add the *ending* (suffix) 'ing' to a word.

Rules for Adding the Suffix 'ing'

1. Adding 'ing' to a **short vowel** word:

Make sure the vowel 'i' in 'ing' will not make a short vowel long. If that happens, you must **double the consonant to protect the short vowel.**

hop   hopping

short 'o'

  You can think of the consonants as body guards that will protect the short vowel. Remember, you need **two** body guards!

VCV
hop   hoping   hopping

short 'o'   long 'o'   short 'o'

 In many exercises, the image of the body guards will be present to remind the student to **protect the short vowel**.

 ★ The consonants below are **never** doubled: ★

c h j k q v w x y

bo<u>x</u> - bo<u>x</u>ing   fi<u>x</u> - fi<u>x</u>ing

Rules for Adding the Suffix 'ing' (continued)

2. Adding 'ing' to a word ending with 'e':

   drop the 'e' and add the 'ing'

   tāpe   tāping

   one letter jump - 'a' is long

   For all other words, just add the 'ing'.

 In many exercises, the image of the Karate kick will be present to remind the student to omit the "silent" 'e'.

Short vowel words that need protecting:

ship - shi**pp**ing   win - wi**nn**ing

rid - ri**dd**ing   hit - hi**tt**ing

Need 2 body guards!

Words that end with 'e':

take - taking   wake - waking

hike - hiking   bite - biting

Get rid of the 'e'!

All other words:

pack - packing   risk - risking

try - trying   boat - boating

plant - planting   eat - eating

rent - renting   sleep - sleeping

Just add 'ing'

Since the overall goal of this program is to teach reading, adding a suffix to **multi-syllable** words is not addressed.

* For words with multiple syllables, if the last syllable is not primary (not stressed) then you do **not** double the last consonant.

Exercise 20.1

Fill in the vowel pairs for the common long vowel teams.

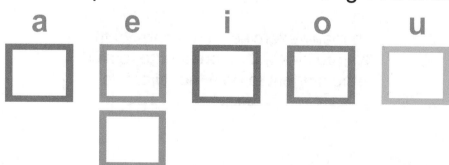

Exercise 20.2
Choose the words that make sense, and then add the ending 'ing' to the words to complete the sentences.

1. The boy was _____ the nail with a hammer.
   pet   hit

2. The girl was _____ into a hamburger.
   bite   dive

3. I was _____ to see you later.
   hope   like

4. The rabbit was _____ away from us.
   sit   hop

5. The woman was _____ a drink.
   sip   mop

Exercise 20.3
Complete the words below.

1.   tr__ __

2.   p__ __

3.   sn__ k__

4.   t__p__

5.   t__ __l

6.   tr__ __n

7.   p__ __l

8.   t__ __

Exercise 20.4
Add 'ing' to the words below. **+ ing**

1. take _____   5. pet _____

2. part _____   6. like _____

3. cry _____   7. melt _____

4. sit _____   8. sing _____

Exercise 20.5
Circle the letters that make the sound indicated on the left. There may be one or two answers.

1. What makes a long 'a' ?	ay	igh	ai
2. What makes a long 'e' ?	ee	oy	ea
3. What makes a long 'i' ?	igh	ie	oi
4. What makes a long 'o' ?	oo	oa	oy
5. What makes a long 'u' ?	ue	oy	ou

Assign the dictations for this lesson.
Also, at this point your student should begin reading books with a partner using the "side-by-side" reading method described in this book.

Review
Lessons 11-20

1) Review the flash cards.
2) Check the dictations from the previous lesson.

 Read the words below.

stool	flinch	starter	spew	loan
shook	try	about	fine	jail
quite	high	cow	feel	flying
quiet	coin	grow	treat	stopping

Exercise R2.1
Read and complete the sentences below.

1. The boy grew an i __ __ __ last year.

2. Carrots, peas and beef are used to make st__ __.

3. The playset had a swing and a sl__ __ __.

4. Trees are planted in the gr__ __ __ __.

5. Cars and trucks can drive on the r__ __ __.

Exercise R2.2
Circle the words that are correctly spelled and read them out loud.

1. shirt / shurt   4. were / wer

2. stor / store   5. turn / tirn

3. therd / third   6. ferst / first

Exercise R2.3
Write the words for each picture below.

VCV Words

1. _____

2. _____

3. _____

4. _____

5. _____

6. _____

VV Words

7. _____

8. _____

9. _____

10. _____

11. _____

12. 3 _____

Exercise R2.4

Read the sentences and circle the words that have the correct vowel teams for the long 'e' sound.

1. I <u>feel / feal</u> sick today.

2. If it is not fake, then it is <u>reel / real</u>.

3. There are seven days in a <u>week / weak</u>.

4. At night we go to <u>sleep / sleap</u>.

5. My house is just down the <u>street / streat</u>.

Exercise R2.5

Compete the sentences below.

1. The horse is in the b___ ___n.

2. The farmer grew a lot of c___ ___n.

3. At night we wish on a st___ ___.

4. There is nothing inside the j___ ___.

5. The red b___ ___ was in my hair.

6. The sp___ ___n is next to the bowl.

7. You must sweep the floor with the br___ ___m.

8. The king always wore a cr___ ___n.

Exercise R2.6

Complete each sentence by adding the word for what the pictures are doing. For all words you will have to add 'ing'.

+ing

 1. The boy is _____.

 2. The hands are _____.

 3. The baby is _____.

 4. The deer is _____.

 5. The dog is _____.

 6. The man is _____.

 Review all lessons up to this point using the on-line games.

When reading past tense words,
they don't always sound the way they're spelled.

Sounds Like It's Spelled

handed
rested
listed
hated
} /ed/

Does NOT Sound Like It's Spelled

jumped
shopped
hopped
wished
} /t/ or /d/

If the word ends with a /t/ or /d/ sound, then you **hear** the /ed/, which adds another syllable to the word.

The words that do **not** end with /t/ or /d/ do **not** get another syllable; and the end sound is just a /d/ or /t/ sound added to the end of the word.

Read the words below.

lasted	crowded	inflated
waited	sounded	stated
kicked	parked	sipped
ruled	boiled	planned

Read the following sentences:

1. The flavor of the gum lasted a long time.
2. We camped out at the beach last summer.
3. They waited a long time to see the show.
4. Jim jumped up onto the couch.
5. Jan turned around and clapped her hands.

Exercise 21.1
Circle the ending sound for each word.

1. clapped   /t/ or /ed/   6. wished   /t/ or /ed/

2. twisted   /t/ or /ed/   7. flashed   /t/ or /ed/

3. shopped   /t/ or /ed/   8. kicked   /t/ or /ed/

4. flopped   /t/ or /ed/   9. rested   /t/ or /ed/

5. clicked   /t/ or /ed/   10. handed   /t/ or /ed/

Rules for Adding 'ed'

1. You may have to double a consonant
to protect a short vowel.

hop   hop<u>p</u>ed

2. If the word ends with a *consonant* followed by
a 'y', turn the 'y' to an 'i' and then add the 'ed'.

'y' to 'i'

cr<u>y</u>   cr<u>i</u>ed

3. If the word ends with an 'e', just add the 'd'.

hop<u>e</u>   hop<u>ed</u>

Exercise 21.2
Write the words below in their **past tense** form. **+ ed**

1. skip   _____

2. shop   _____

3. plan   _____

4. rip   _____

5. drag   _____

Don't forget us!

Words that end with a consonant followed by a 'y'

In words with a consonant
followed by 'y',
turn the 'y' to 'i'.
But here's the thing,
don't do this for /ing/.

spy

spied

spying

Exercise 21.3

Read the sentences and write the missing words in the correct tense (past or present) on the lines.

1. The boy is __ __ __ __ __ __.
   cry

2. The sad girl __ __ __ __ __ last night.
   cry

3. He __ __ __ __ __ to open the jar.
   try

4. She was __ __ __ __ __ __ to read to the boy.
   try

5. They ate __ __ __ __ __ chicken for dinner.
   fry

6. The fish was __ __ __ __ __ __ in the pan.
   fry

Irregular Past Tense Verbs

Below are *some* past tense words that are different, or irregular. Here, 'ed' is **not** added.

wake - woke	take - took	sleep - slept
run - ran	shake - shook	eat - ate
sing - sang	stink - stunk	sit - sat

Use the sentence below to help identify irregular past tense verbs.

Today I _____, but yesterday I _____.

"Today I <u>sing,</u> but yesterday I <u>sang</u>."

Exercise 21.4
Draw lines to match each word to its **past tense** form.

1.	eat		took
2.	make		flew
3.	shake		dug
4.	fly		ate
5.	draw		kept
6.	take		drew
7.	keep		shook
8.	dig		made

Exercise 21.5

Circle the words that make sense, and then write the past tense form of the words on the lines.

1. He _____ at the bug with a stick.
　　　　　　sit　　　　poke

2. The children _____ in the snow.
　　　　　　　　eat　　　　play

3. We _____ for the bus to pick us up.
　　　　wait　　　dream

4. We _____ the fish swim in the tank.
　　　　watch　　　drop

5. Yesterday, my mother _____ a cake.
　　　　　　　　　　bake　　　lick

6. I went to get my hair _____ .
　　　　　　　　　pick　　　trim

Assign the dictations for this lesson,
and have your student play the on-line games below for this
lesson as well as prior lessons that need review.

Blast Off　　　　　Save the Earth
Matching Game　　　Reading Game

1) Review the flash cards.
2) Check the dictations from the previous lesson.

nd

and

end

ind

ond

und

* All vowels are short except for 'ind' where the 'i' is **usually** long.

b<u>and</u>	p<u>ond</u>
s<u>end</u>	<u>und</u>er
k<u>ind</u>	

 Read the words below.

find	thunder	mixing	glue	taking
behind	blunder	fixing	blue	sleeping
remind	standing	boxing	cube	growing
blind	spending	soaked	tube	flying

'ild' Words

The 'i', in the three words below, has the long 'i' sound.

w<u>i</u>ld   ch<u>i</u>ld   m<u>i</u>ld

Are you a <u>wild</u> <u>child</u>, or a <u>mild</u> <u>child</u>?

Exercise 22.1

Fill in the blanks to complete the words in the sentences below.

> and   end   ind   ond   und

1. I would rather sit than st__ __ __.

2. Ducks and fish swim in the p__ __ __.

3. I need to f__ __ __ my suitcase for the trip.

4. Look __ __ __er the bed for your socks.

5. I sp__ __ __ a lot of time at school.

Exercise 22.2

Circle the words that make sense for the sentences below.

1. We're / Were going to send the letter today.

2. She said we're / were leaving at the end of June.

3. We where / were staying over his house for dinner.

4. Were / Where the children hiding under the blankets?

5. Were / Where are the birds finding food in the winter?

Exercise 22.3
Circle the answer to the questions below.

What letters make...

1. the long 'o' sound?   oi   oa

2. the long 'o' sound?   ow   oi

3. the /ou/ sound as in "ouch"?   oi   ow

4. the long 'a' sound?   ie   ai

5. the long 'a' sound?   ay   oa

6. the long 'i' sound?   igh   oi

Exercise 22.4
Complete the sentences so that they make sense.

1. She _____ the nametag onto his shirt.
   pin

2. The girl was _____ down the street.
   run

3. The boy _____ into the pool.
   jump

4. The pilot _____ the plane on the runway.
   land

5. The girls were _____ the game.
   win

Exercise 22.5
Circle the words that have the long 'i' sound (there are 6).

fly	child	list	winning	find
sight	shin	wild	cry	mint

Exercise 22.6
Circle the words that are correctly spelled.

1. rane / rain   6. return / retern

2. shirt / shurt   7. clowd / cloud

3. jumpt / jumped   8. town / toun

4. hurt / hirt   9. were / wer

5. shopt / shopped   10. street / streat

Exercise 22.7
In the letter groups below, underline the vowels that are long due to the **V**V or **V**CV long vowel rules (there are 3).

gidde   smitbe   bito

higip   guebt   anpe

Assign the dictations for this lesson,
and have your student play the on-line games for review.

The /ct/ Sounds

1) Review the flash cards.
2) Check the dictations from the previous lesson.

Note: use the **phonics reference chart** on the back cover of this book to review older sounds.

The 'ct' sound comes quick and is usually in larger words.

ct

act

ect

ict

oct

uct

All
vowels
are
short.

p<u>act</u>

obj<u>ect</u>

pred<u>ict</u>

<u>Oct</u>ober

instr<u>uct</u>

 Read the words below.

fact	doctor	milder	boiler
factor	octagon	wilder	soil
impact	construct	child	grown
effect	tractor	children	gown
reject	spectator	reminder	shouted

Exercise 23.1
Complete the sentences with the sounds below. Sounds may be used more than once or not at all.

> act   ect   ict   oct   uct

1. Conn___ ___ ___ the dots.

2. The man will be ___ ___ ___ing in the play.

3. You can sel___ ___ ___ where we go for dinner.

4. She says that she can pred___ ___ ___ what will happen.

5. The woman is a susp___ ___ ___ in the crime.

6. The loud man was ej___ ___ ___ed from the game.

Exercise 23.2
Circle the words that make sense. Be careful; sometimes a past tense word sounds like a 'ct' word.

1. The dog lict / licked my hand.

2. The car bact / backed down the driveway.

3. The boys made a pact / packed to always be friends.

4. She dropped the cup on the floor and it cract / cracked.

Exercise 23.3
Complete the sentences below so that they make sense.

1. The boy _____ on the banana peel.
   slip

2. The girl _____ to look over the railing.
   try

3. The child _____ an object on the beach.
   find

4. The boy _____ mean to us.
   act

5. The dog was _____ away from the girl.
   run

6. The dirty boy _____ a bubble bath in the tub.
   take

7. The children _____ on the teachers.
   spy

8. The child _____ down the road.
   skip

9. We _____ up our things for the trip.
   pack

10. The bird _____ away from us.
    fly

Exercise 23.4

Read the sentences and circle the matching pictures.

1. The teacher good, but she is strict.

2. He is the conductor

3. The farmer rides on a tractor.

4. The man will collect our trash.

5. The inspector looked for clues.

6. The doctor helped the sick man.

7. An insect landed on my hand.

Assign the dictations for this lesson, and have your student play the on-line games for review.

Lesson 24 — The 'aw', 'au', 'all' and 'alk' Sounds

1) Review the flash cards.
2) Check the dictations from the previous lesson.

1

There are two ways to get the /aw/ sound.

p<u>aw</u>   str<u>aw</u>   cl<u>aw</u>   j<u>aw</u>

2

f<u>au</u>lt   l<u>au</u>nch   h<u>au</u>nt   h<u>au</u>l

Point out that 'aw' is usually at the **end** of a word, and 'au' is usually in the **middle** of a word.

Read the words below.

law	vault	join	pout	sound
draw	fault	joist	spout	found
saw	author	hoist	clout	around

strict	doctor	inspect	kind	fruit
effect	collect	select	find	suit
actor	reject	instruct	mind	ruin

Exercise 24.1
Draw lines to match the words to their pictures.

1. crawl

2. saw

3. paw

4. draw

5. haunt

6. claw

7. straw

8. yawn

'all' has the /awl/ sound.

/awl/

t<u>all</u>   w<u>all</u>   f<u>all</u>   b<u>all</u>   c<u>all</u>

'alk' has the /awk/ sound.

/awk/

t<u>alk</u>   w<u>alk</u>   ch<u>alk</u>   st<u>alk</u>   b<u>alk</u>

Exercise 24.2
Draw lines to match the words to their pictures.

1. ball

2. wall

3. fall

4. walk

5. talk

6. chalk

Exercise 24.3
Complete the sentences with the words that make sense.

walk   ball   awful   pause   fault

1. It was my _____ we were late for the show.

2. She likes to _____ her dog down the street.

3. The dog chased the _____ that I threw.

4. Burnt toast smells _____.

5. You can stop the song by pressing _____.

Exercise 24.4
Draw lines to match the sounds.

1. igh   ai

2. aw   oi

3. oy   oo

4. ew   er

5. ay   ie

6. ur   au

Exercise 24.5
Complete the sentences with the words that make sense.

because	lawn	launch	dawn
subject	predict	author	drawn

1. The _____ wrote a book about animals.

2. I like baseball _____ it is fun!

3. My best _____ is math.

4. The opposite of dusk is _____ .

5. I tried to _____ what will happen next.

6. My father has to mow the _____ .

7. We went to the _____ to watch the rocket blast off.

Assign the dictations for this lesson,
and have your student play the on-line games below for this lesson as well as prior lessons that need review.

Blast Off
Matching Game

Save the Earth
Reading Game

happy

1) Review the flash cards.
2) Check the dictations from the previous lesson.

Very often, the letter 's' sounds like /z/.
Also, words ending with /s/ or /z/
usually end with a "do nothing" 'e'.

s = /z/ ➡ please   noise   raise

s = /s/ ➡ horse   goose   sense

Exercise 25.1
Draw lines to match the words to their pictures.

1. toes

2. nose

3. pose

4. rose

5. hose

Exercise 25.2
Fill in the missing letters to complete the words below.

1. h__ __ __ __

3. n__ __ __ __

2. h__ __ __ __

4. m__ __ __ __

Exercise 25.3
Circle the words that make sense in the sentences below.

1. The mouse / blouse took the cheese from the trap.

2. It is polite to say pause / please and thank you.

3. It is fun to ride on a house / horse.

4. My house / horse is just around the block.

5. My loud brother made a lot of nose / noise.

6. She chose / choose to go home at nine o'clock.

7. They will use the lid to clues / close the jar.

Exercise 25.4
Complete the sentences below so that they make sense.

1. The boy is _____ soap to wash his hands.
    use

2. The girl _____ when her dog was lost.
    cry

3. We _____ the map to get around town.
    use

4. They _____ our car at the border.
    stop

5. I am _____ and locking the door.
    close

Exercise 25.5
Circle the **seven** words below where the 's' has the /z/ sound.

these	use	chase
those	his	wise
case	nurse	crease
house	purse	pause
horse	because	loose

Exercise 25.6
Complete the sentences below so that they make sense.

1. The mouse _____ its way out of the box.
   claw

2. The snake _____ up and hissed at us.
   coil

3. I had a hard time _____ a good song to sing.
   choose

4. The boy was _____ like he knew what to do.
   act

5. The child _____ behind the bush.
   crawl

Exercise 25.7
Circle the matching sounds; there is one per line.

1. aw	oa	ai	au
2. oi	oy	ou	aw
3. oo	oa	ew	ow
4. ou	ow	oi	ue
5. ie	ai	ew	igh

Assign the dictations for this lesson,
and have your student play the on-line games for review.

The Letter 'y'

The letter 'y' can function as a vowel *and* a consonant.

The **sound** that 'y' makes,
depends on **where** it is in a word.

1 If a word **starts** with the letter 'y', it has
the *consonant* sound /y/ as in "yellow".

yell   yes   yard

2 If 'y' is in the **middle** of a word,
it acts like the vowel 'i'.

myth   style

short 'i'   long 'i'

3 If 'y' is at the **end** of a word,
it acts like a long 'i' or long 'e'.

cry   happy

long 'i'   long 'e'

'y' acts like a vowel

Show how the 'y' turned the 'i' long.

tin
tiny
↑ long 'i'

fun
funny
↑ short 'u'

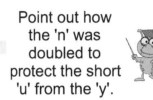
Point out how the 'n' was doubled to protect the short 'u' from the 'y'.

 Read the words below.

yarn	system	hurry	cry
yell	symbol	funny	try
yummy	mystery	crazy	supply
young	type	lazy	satisfy
yellow	style	happy	deny

Exercise 26.1

Circle the words that make sense in the sentences.

1. What type / crazy of pie is your favorite?

2. The brown blanket is ugly but it is funny / cozy.

3. I went to the bakery / pantry to buy donuts.

4. We had to supply / deny the camp with food and water.

5. Try not to be noisy / silly when people are sleeping.

6. The creepy / sneaky dog stole meat from the young boy.

7. It is a mystery / symbol where the candy went.

Exercise 26.2

Draw lines to match the words to their pictures.

1. lady

2. pony

3. monkey

4. money

5. baby

6. itchy

7. key

8. fly

9. spy

10. cry

At the **end** of a word, 'y' can sound like a long ____ or a long ____.

Exercise 26.3

Circle the words that make sense in the sentences below.

1.   The haunted house was crunchy / scary.

2.   I cannot deny / supply that I ate the peach pie.

3.   I have to comply / rely on my lungs to breathe.

4.   We waited for the paint to modify / dry.

5.   The meal did not satisfy / supply my hunger.

6.   He tried to pry / dry the lid off the jar.

7.   We got party / plenty of rain last September.

8.   We have to worry / hurry to catch the airplane.

9.   We had to modify / classify our plans for dinner.

10. The crazy / lazy monkey ran off with my yellow hat.

In the **middle** of a word, 'y' can sound like a long ___ or a short ___.

Assign the dictations for this lesson, and have your student play the on-line games for review.

1) Review the flash cards.
2) Check the dictations from the previous lesson.

ly

ly = /lee/

The suffix (ending) 'ly' sounds like /lee/,
where 'y' has the long 'e' sound.

happy - happi<u>ly</u>

sad - sad<u>ly</u>

quick - quick<u>ly</u>

* Notice how the 'y' in "happy" got changed to an 'i'.

Adding a Suffix (ending)
In words with a consonant followed by 'y',
turn the 'y' to 'i'. But here's the thing,
don't do this for /ing/.

For words that **end** with '**le**',
take out the 'e' and add the 'y'.

simp<u>le</u>   simp<u>ly</u>

Read the words below.

close - close<u>ly</u>   instant - instant<u>ly</u>

slow - slow<u>ly</u>   merry - merri<u>ly</u>

sick - sick<u>ly</u>   lazy - lazi<u>ly</u>

Exercise 27.1
Add the ending 'ly' to the words below.

+ ly

1. _____
   normal

2. _____
   final

3. _____
   safe

4. _____
   lucky

5. _____
   angry

6. _____
   happy

Exercise 27.2
Circle the words that make sense in the sentences below.

1. We quietly tip-toed through the <u>library / kangaroo</u>.

2. The baby quickly grabbed his <u>mailbox / bottle</u>.

3. The cook slowly stirred the <u>soup / donkey</u>.

4. The singer softly sang a <u>bagel / song</u>.

5. He really likes to eat turkey <u>sandwiches / baskets</u>.

We saw the 'er' sound in an earlier lesson, but here we show how we can *change* a word by adding 'er' to the *end.*

'i' sounds like a long 'e'

happy - happi<u>er</u>

Turn 'y' (after a consonant) to 'i', then add 'er'.

sad - sadd<u>er</u>

Protect your short vowel!

quick - quick<u>er</u>

Just add 'er'.

 Read the words below.

saf<u>e</u> - saf<u>er</u>　　　　sick - sick<u>er</u>

slow - slow<u>er</u>　　　　fat - fatt<u>er</u>

eas<u>y</u> - eas<u>ier</u>　　　　trick<u>y</u> - trick<u>ier</u>

Read the following sentences:

1. His new car is shiny, but her new car is shinier.
2. Yesterday was foggy, but today it is foggier.
3. Your fried chicken is crispier than mine.
4. Today will be sunnier than yesterday.
5. My uncle is funnier than my father.

Exercise 27.3
Add the ending 'er' to the words below.

+ er

1. hot   _____

2. big   _____

3. fat   _____

4. hit   _____

5. jog   _____

Exercise 27.4
Add the ending 'er' to the words below.

+ er

1. happy   _____

2. funny   _____

3. ugly   _____

4. sorry   _____

5. pretty   _____

Assign the dictations for this lesson,
and have your student play the on-line games for review.

1) Review the flash cards.

2) Check the dictations from the previous lesson.

Note that up to this point, 'g' has had a hard /g/ sound, as in "get". Now we'll see when 'g' has the soft /j/ sound, as in "gem".

Rule 1

When 'g' is followed by an **'e'**, **'i'** or **'y'** it *sometimes* has the /j/ sound.

g (sometimes) = /j/ when: g<u>e</u>   g<u>i</u>   g<u>y</u>

Rule 2

There are **no** words in the English language that end with the **letter 'j'**.

Words that end with the /j/ sound, **<u>must</u>** end with a '**ge**'.

ge gi gy

char<u>ge</u>   <u>gi</u>ant   aller<u>gy</u>

 Read the words below.

ca<u>ge</u>   sta<u>ge</u>   ener<u>gy</u>   lar<u>ge</u>   hu<u>ge</u>

pa<u>ge</u>   <u>gi</u>st   din<u>gy</u>   stin<u>gy</u>   <u>gi</u>gantic

Exercise 28.1

Circle the sound that the 'ge', 'gi' or 'gy' makes in the words below. If you don't know, try the 'g' as a /g/ and a /j/.

1. g<u>e</u>m   /j/ or /g/

2. g<u>i</u>rl   /j/ or /g/

3. hun<u>ge</u>r   /j/ or /g/

4. dan<u>ge</u>r   /j/ or /g/

Rule 3

For short vowel words, you must protect the short vowel with a 'd'.

Now you have two body guards!

<u>d</u>ge

The 'd' acts as a body guard to protect the short vowel.

All first vowels are short.

| adge | edge | idge | odge | udge |

b<u>adge</u>   pl<u>edge</u>   br<u>idge</u>   d<u>odge</u>   b<u>udge</u>

 Read the words below.

badger   fridge   judge   grudge

wedge   lodge   smudge   fudge

Exercise 28.2
Circle the sounds that make real words.

1. j _?_   udge   adge   5. pl _?_   edge   idge

2. br _?_   edge   idge   6. b _?_   adge   edge

3. l _?_   edge   adge   7. w _?_   adge   edge

4. sl _?_   adge   udge   8. gr _?_   udge   adge

Exercise 28.3
Fill in the blanks with the words that make sense in the sentences.

wedge   judge   stage   edge   huge

1. The actor walked up on the _____.

2. Another word for "big" is _____.

3. The diver stood on the _____ of the cliff.

4. I'll have a _____ of cheddar cheese.

5. In a court-room, you will find a _____.

A common sound that ends with /j/ is: **nge**

The 'a' in "ange" is *usually* long, all other first vowels are short.

<u>a</u>nge   enge   inge   onge   unge

r<u>ange</u>   chall<u>enge</u>   b<u>inge</u>   c<u>onge</u>st   l<u>unge</u>

 Read the words below.

change   danger   hinge   plunge

strange   stranger   revenge   fringe

Exercise 28.4
Circle the word that makes sense for each sentence.

1. Emily is <u>plunging / changing</u> into her bathing suit.

2. Her job is to <u>arrange / plunge</u> the flowers in the vase.

3. The angry man said he would get <u>napkins/ revenge</u>.

4. They said that we should not talk to <u>strangers / dangers</u>.

5. The lines come together to make an <u>angel / angle</u>.

6. When the ball came at me, I <u>cringed / plunged</u>.

Exercise 28.5
Circle the sounds that make real words.

1. cr__?__   ange   inge

2. arr__?__   ange   inge

3. str__?__   ange   inge

4. tw__?__   ange   inge

5. pl__?__   unge   inge

6. l__?__   unge   inge

7. b__?__   unge   inge

8. fr__?__   unge   inge

Exercise 28.6
Complete the words below.

1. f__ __ __ __

2. pl __ __ __ er

3.  an__ __ __

4. fr__ __ __ __

5. br__ __ __ __

6.  b __ __ __ __

Assign the dictations for this lesson, and have your student play the on-line game "'g' as /j/".

When 'c' has the /s/ Sound

1) Review the flash cards.

2) Check the dictations from the previous lesson.

Note that up to this point, 'c' has had a hard /k/ sound, as in "cat". Now we'll see when 'c' has the soft /s/ sound, as in "city".

Rule

When 'c' is followed by an '**e**', '**i**' or '**y**' it *always* has the /s/ sound.

c = /s/ when: c<u>e</u>   c<u>i</u>   c<u>y</u>

dan<u>ce</u>   <u>ci</u>rcle   fan<u>cy</u>

Read the words below.

cent	percent	force
centimeter	recent	pencil
circle	decent	choice

/s/

pen<u>ci</u>l

Tell your students that the same letters change the 'c' to /s/ as the 'g' to /j/.

ge
gi } /j/ *sometimes*
gy

ce
ci } /s/ *always*
cy

All first vowels are short.

ance   ence   ince   once   unce

d<u>ance</u>   sci<u>ence</u>   s<u>ince</u>   sc<u>once</u>   d<u>unce</u>

 Read the words below.

prance	chance	fence
trance	glance	wince
stance	hence	prince

face	place	price	spice
race	lace	slice	space
trace	mice	advice	twice

Exercise 29.1
Circle the words that make sense in the sentences below.

1. What <u>percent / advice</u> of three hundred is fifty-five?

2. What <u>circle / advice</u> did the lady give you?

3. What is the <u>dance / chance</u> of rain for today?

4. Where is the best <u>place / space</u> to hang my coat?

5. Why was the <u>choice / price</u> of the fruit so high?

Exercise 29.2

Circle the sounds that make a real word. There may be more than one correct answer for each line.

1. pl__?__   ace   ice

2. f__?__   ace   ice

3. r__?__   ace   ice

4. sp__?__   ace   ice

5. gr__?__   ace   ice

6. sl__?__   ace   ice

7. adv__?__   ace   ice

8. p__?__   ace   ice

Exercise 29.3

Circle the sounds that make a real word. There may be more than one correct answer for each line.

1. gl__?__   ance   ange

2. ch__?__   ance   ange

3. pr__?__   ance   ange

4. r__?__   ance   ange

5. tr__?__   ance   ange

Exercise 29.4

Complete the words in the sentences below using the sounds in the box.

Sounds may be used more than once.

ice	ace	ance	ence	ince

1. The boy ran in the r_____.

2. I ordered a sl_____ of peach pie.

3. My mouth and nose are part of my f_____.

4. I have not seen him s_____ last year.

5. The rocket blasted off into sp_____.

6. We enjoyed watching the lady d_____.

7. The new teacher was very n_____ to me.

8. The f_____ keeps our dog in the yard.

9. Asking others for adv_____ makes sense.

10. Pl_____ your belongings into the bag.

Exercise 29.5
Complete the sentences below so that they make sense.

1. The lady was _____ on the stage.

dance

2. The girl _____ a gift in the mail.

receive

3. The deer _____ around the woods.

prance

4. The player was _____ to the next level.

advance

5. The child _____ the image on the paper.

trace

Exercise 29.6
Circle the four words below where 'g' sounds like /j/.

raged	forged	energy	get
bagged	foggy	clingy	gerbil

Assign the dictations for this lesson, and have your student play the 'c' as /s/ on-line games (there are three activities and a review of the rule).

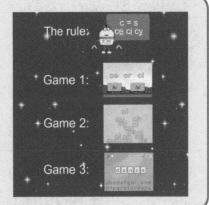

'c' or 'k' for /k/

If 'c' makes the /k/ sound and 'k' makes the /k/ sound, which one do I use?

Rule: When to Use 'c' or 'k'

Always use 'c' for the /k/ sound UNLESS

1. the /k/ sound is followed by an 'e', 'i' or 'y', or
2. the /k/ sound is at the end of a one syllable word,

then you must use 'k'.

In the words below, /k/ is followed by 'e', 'i' or 'y', so we use 'k' for the /k/ sound.

keep	king
kept	sky
kit	skip

If we used 'c', then we would not have /k/, we would have /s/ instead.

According to rule #2, we always use a 'k' at the end of a **one syllable** word ending with /k/.

duc<u>k</u>   bric<u>k</u>   stac<u>k</u>   luc<u>k</u>

Okay, use 'k' for the /k/ sound at the end of one syllable words. What about **two** syllable words that end with /k/?

 Two (or more) syllable words that end with /k/ *usually* end with 'ic':

pan<u>ic</u>   top<u>ic</u>   traff<u>ic</u>   bas<u>ic</u>

 Read the words below.

music	logic	picnic	critic	volcanic
mimic	lyric	traffic	ironic	frolic
panic	cubic	tragic	hectic	comic

Read the following sentences:

1. I put the traffic ticket into my pocket.

2. Do not panic if the plastic dish gets lost.

3. On Sunday, we will have a picnic with our friends.

4. The bird will mimic the way you talk.

5. We listened to the music all night.

Exercise 30.1

Read the words to your student and have him/her use the /k/ rule to determine the correct way to spell each word.

1.	skill	scill	5.	piknik	picnic
2.	kind	cind	6.	keep	ceep
3.	klap	clap	7.	klear	clear
4.	traffik	traffic	8.	kamp	camp

Exercise 30.2

Fill in the boxes with the sound that each 'c' makes and then read the word out loud.

'k' or 's'

1. □□ accent

2. □ bounce

3. □ mercy

4. □□ accident

5. □□ success

6. □□ accept

Exercise 30.3

Complete the sentences with the words that make sense.

fantastic	plastic	traffic	attic
romantic	garlic	magic	panic

1. We found the kitten hiding up in the _____.

2. The cook chopped the _____.

3. Do not _____ if you are in an accident.

4. Terrific and _____ mean the same thing.

5. The _____ toy easily broke.

6. My parents went out for a _____ dinner.

7. There was a lot of _____ on the highway.

8. We saw a _____ show at school today.

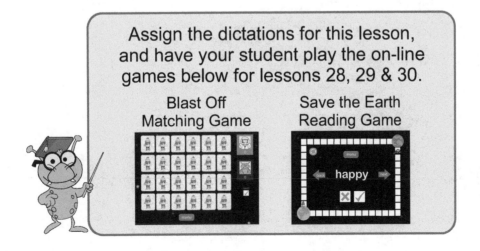

Assign the dictations for this lesson, and have your student play the on-line games below for lessons 28, 29 & 30.

Blast Off Matching Game   Save the Earth Reading Game

Review
Lessons 21-30

1) Review the flash cards.
2) Check the dictations from the previous lesson.

 Read the words below.

tried	pause	mystery	prince
find	because	system	price
doctor	happier	slowly	circle
law	funnier	giant	traffic

Exercise R3.1
Match the sounds on the left with the sounds on the right.

1. ce   /aw/

2. au   /awl/

3. adge   /aj/

4. alk   /s/

5. all   /awk/

Exercise R3.2
Complete the crossword puzzle.

pause

fault

claws

predict

false

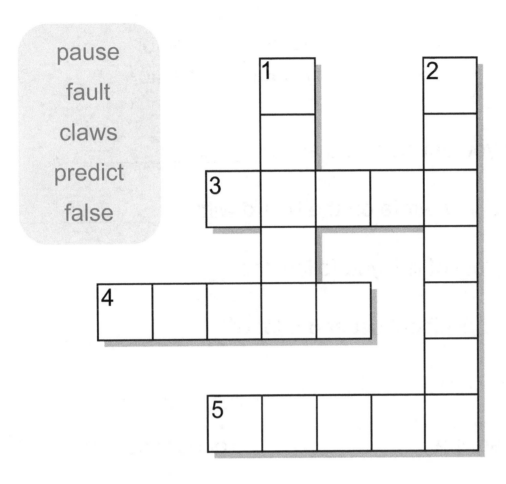

Down

1. A cat has sharp __.

2. A fortune teller may __ the future.

Across

3. You can play, __ or stop a video.

4. If it is not true, then it is __ .

5. Do not blame me, it is not my __ .

Exercise R3.3
Complete the sentences with the words that make sense.

law	talk	doctor
chalk	symbol	traffic

1. When you get sick, you see a _____.

2. The teacher wrote on the board with _____.

3 To stay out of jail, you follow the _____.

4. The car accident caused a lot of _____.

5. Another word for "chat" is _____.

6. The flag is a _____ of our country.

Exercise R3.4
Answer the questions below.

1. 'g' *sometimes* is /j/ when followed by: ___ ___ ___

2. 'c' *always* is /s/ when followed by: ___ ___ ___

3. When 'y' is in the **middle** of a word, it can sound like:

long ____ or short ____

4. When 'y' is at the **end** of a word it can sound like:

long ____ or long ____

Exercise R3.5
Fill in the blanks to spell the words for the pictures below.

1. j __ __ __ __

2. c __ __ __

3. b __ __ __ __

4. br __ __ __ __

5. b __ __ n __ __

6. pen __ __ __

7. 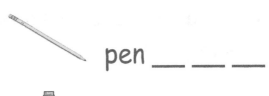 jui __ __

8. pr __ __ __

Exercise R3.6
Add 'ly' to the words and write the new word on the line.

+ ly

1. soft _____

2. swift _____

3. late _____

4. easy _____

5. final _____

6. lucky _____

Exercise R3.7
Complete the sentences with the words that make sense.

choice	space	principal	chance
force	city	fence	race

1. The drawer does not have a lot of _____ for all of my socks.

2. There is a sixty percent _____ of rain for today.

3. Do not _____ me to go out when I am sick.

4. Every year we go to the _____ to see a show.

5. The large dog jumped over the _____ .

6. Our teacher gave us a _____ on what to do for homework.

7. The _____ of our school is very strict.

8. The _____ car zoomed around the track.

Review all lessons up to this point using the on-line games.

Review the flash cards, and check any dictations that may need to be checked.

Before proceedings, you may want to explain to your student what a **noun** is.

The word "plural" means more than one.
Usually, you can just add 's' when making a noun plural.

1

dog - dog<u>s</u>

But for words that end with: /s/, /z/, /sh/, /ch/, and /x/, you must add an 'es'.

watch - watch<u>es</u>

2

You can <u>hear</u> this when you say it!

And if a word ends with 'f' or 'fe', usually the 'f' or 'fe' comes out and is replaced with a 'ves'.

loaf - loa<u>ves</u>

3

You can also <u>hear</u> this when you say it!

If a word ends with a consonant followed by a 'y',
turn the 'y' to an 'i' and add 'es':

4 **baby - babies**

Adding a Suffix to Words Ending with 'y'

Remember to add an ending (suffix):

In words like spy,
turn the 'y' to an 'i'.
But here's the thing,
don't do this for /ing/.

 This rule is only for words that end with a consonant followed by a 'y', like the word "spy".

supply**ing** ← 'y' stays when adding 'ing'

suppl**ier**
suppl**ied** } 'y' changes to 'i'
suppl**ies**

Irregular Plural Nouns

Many plural nouns don't get the 's' at all!
Listed below are only some of these words.

man - men   foot - feet

woman - women   tooth - teeth

child - children   mouse - mice

Exercise 31.1
First read the words in the box below. Then complete the sentences with the **plural form** of the words that make sense.

> house - houses   lady - ladies
> box - boxes   cherry - cherries
> lash - lashes   try - tries
> wolf - wolves   puppy - puppies

1. The boy stacked the _____ on the shelf.

2. The girl had long eye- _____ .

3. The _____ roamed the hills in packs.

4. There were a lot of _____ in the litter.

5. How many _____ are on your block?

6. We picked a bunch of _____ from the tree.

7. All of the _____ came over for lunch.

8. They gave us three _____ to pass the test.

Remind your student that 'x' does not get doubled to protect short vowels.

box - boxed - boxing - boxes

Exercise 31.2

For each sentence, choose the word that make sense and then make the word plural.

1. How many _____ to you need for packing?

                      box   frog

2. There are seven _____ in a week.

                      insect   day

3. In the fall, we had to rake the _____ .

                      leaf   nest

4. We were granted three _____ .

                      wish   dish

5. The boy likes bedtime _____ .

                      price   story

Exercise 31.3

Read the hints below, and then circle the words that the hints describe.

1. When you do not know something, it is a __.

        story   fact   mystery

2. If you do not know someone, they are a __.

        stranger   person   stringer

3. Some people may offer you __.

        advise   advance   advice

4. Birds often eat __.

        burry   berries   berry

Often, when a student sees a word, such as "ladies", (s)he may be confused, not realizing that it comes from a word ending with 'y'. In a later lesson your student will learn the rule breaker 'ie' as a long 'e'. That rule can be applied to these plural words.

Exercise 31.4
Write the words below in their plural form.

1. tax _____

2. bush _____

3. lash _____

4. memory _____

5. story _____

Exercise 31.5
Circle the sounds that the underlined letters make.

1. <u>c</u>akes	/k/	/s/	5. chan<u>g</u>es	/g/	/j/
2. <u>c</u>ities	/k/	/s/	6. be<u>g</u>ins	/g/	/j/
3. chan<u>c</u>es	/k/	/s/	7. oran<u>g</u>es	/g/	/j/
4. picni<u>c</u>s	/k/	/s/	8. char<u>g</u>es	/g/	/j/

Assign the dictations for this lesson, and have your student play the on-line games for review.

1) Review the flash cards.
2) Check the dictations from the previous lesson.

Syllables

A **syllable** is a part of a word where it is naturally divided when pronouncing it.

You can feel syllables, when you open and close your mouth when saying a word.

You can also clap out a word, when hearing where the pieces start and stop.

Say the words and count the syllables.

 fish ☐ 1

 ba|by ☐ 2

 pen|cil ☐ 2

 oc|to|pus ☐ 3

 pump|kin ☐ 2

 ac|ci|dent ☐ 3

Exercise 32.1
Write the number of syllables you hear in the words below.

1. funny ☐   5. arrange ☐

2. yellow ☐   6. hunger ☐

3. smudge ☐   7. energy ☐

4. mystery ☐   8. angrier ☐

FLOSS Words

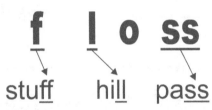

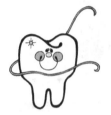

stuff   hill   pass

The word FLOSS is used to remind us to **double** the 'f', 'l' or 's' in words that: have one syllable, have a short vowel, and ends with 'f', 'l' or 's'.

 Read the words below.

cuff	off	tell	glass
stuff	spill	grill	grass
bluff	bell	still	fuss

Exceptions: plus bus gas yes

 Point out how all of these words have only one syllable.

Exercise 32.2

Write the words for the pictures below. Note that all of the words are FLOSS words.

1.  _ _ _ _ _

2.  _ _ _ _ _

3.  _ _ _ _ _ _

4. _ _ _ _ _

5.  _ _ _ _

6.  _ _ _ _

7.  _ _ _ _

8.  _ _ _ _

Two (or more) Syllable Words Ending with /ess/

Words ending with: less, ness, cess or tress, usually end with double 's'!

 Say this like a chant.

 **Read the words below.**

un<u>less</u>	fond<u>ness</u>	suc<u>cess</u>	dis<u>tress</u>
endless	happiness	access	fortress
careless	witness	recess	waitress

Exercise 32.3
Circle the word that makes sense for each sentence.

1. The broken toy was <u>endless / useless</u>.

2. I sleep on a <u>mattress / fortress</u>.

3. The judge called the <u>waitress / witness</u> up to his bench.

4. After lunch, we went outside for <u>success / recess</u>.

5. Do not be <u>careless / skinless</u> when doing your work.

6. When I clean my room, it is <u>distress / spotless</u>.

Long 'o' Words

Below are words that have a long 'o' for no reason.

long 'o'

r<u>oll</u>	poll	troll	volt	colt
toll	scroll	control	bolt	jolt

long 'o'

p<u>ost</u>	most	host	ghost

long 'o'

h<u>old</u>	fold	cold	gold
sold	folder	told	bold

Exercise 32.4
Change the words to their **past tense** forms.

Today I _____, but yesterday I _____.

1. tell   _____

2. hold   _____

3. post   _____

4. fold   _____

5. sell   _____

6. roll   _____

Exercise 32.5
Circle the word that makes sense for each sentence below.

1. The basket holds all of the berries / houses.

2. When it is cold, the store sells many ghosts / scarves.

3. The bus held most of the children / hamburgers.

4. The older ladies like to toss coins into the soil / well.

5. Some **words** in this **sentence** are bowled / bold.

6. It got colder, then we saw the snow flurry / flurries.

Exercise 32.6
Fill in the missing words, using the pictures as clues.

1. The lady is __ __ __.

2. The doctor will __ __ __ __ the baby.

3. You put these on when it is __ __ __ __.

4. The coins were made of __ __ __ __.

5. The papers are in the __ __ __ __ __ __.

6. I like to put butter on my __ __ __ __.

What letters get doubled at the end of a one syllable
word that has a short vowel?
Hint: think of the word "floss"

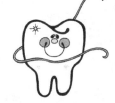

____ ____ ____

Assign the dictations for this lesson,
and have your student play the on-line games for review.

Multi-Syllable Words

1) Review the flash cards.
2) Check the dictations from the previous lesson.

Reading a Long Word

When you see a long word, ask yourself the questions:

Which vowels are long?
Are there consonant blends?
Are there sounds you recognize?
If there is a 'g', can it have the /j/ sound?
If there is a 'c', does it have the /s/ or /k/ sound?

Step 1: Answer the above questions.

Step 2: Break the word up.

Step 3: Sound it out.

Step 4: Change the word, if needed, to be a word you know.

celebrate

Underline any long vowels using the VCV and VV rule.

cel e br ate

Explain how some words do not follow the **V**CV rule. In this word, the first 'e' should be long, but it is short.

For words with more than one syllable, 'age' = /idge/.

message   bandage   baggage

package   average   advantage

For words with more than one syllable, ending
with 'ice' or 'ace', the ending sound is /iss/.

notice   service   palace

justice   practice   necklace

Exercise 33.1
Circle the word that makes sense for each sentence below.

1 He sent a necklace / message that he would be late.

2. The strong boy had the advantage / octopus.

3. I received a lampshade / package in the mail.

4. We loaded our baggage / toenails into the van.

5. To play an instrument well, you must service / practice.

6. Will he justice / notice if we are late?

7. The performer danced on the package / stage.

8. Last year we had an average / message amount of rain.

Exercise 33.2
Write the **long vowel** sounds that are in the words.

1.	kind		6.	most	
2.	right		7.	child	
3.	gold		8.	mild	
4.	roll		9.	wild	
5.	flight		10.	post	

Exercise 33.3
Write the words below in their plural form.

1. story _____

2. lady _____

3. city _____

4. delivery _____

5. family _____

6. factory _____

Exercise 33.4
Circle the words that make sense for the sentences below.

1. In Florida refrigerators / alligators live in swamps.

2. We store our food in the refrigerator / attic.

3. At the medical / amusement park, we went on a roller-coaster.

4. A compound / mythical word is when two words are put together to make one word.

5. His story was not convincing / hindering.

Exercise 33.5
Review: change the words to their **past tense** forms.

1. plan _____   5. wake _____

2. take _____   6. eat _____

3. sell _____   7. go _____

4. run _____   8. hope _____

Assign the dictations for this lesson,
and have your student play the on-line games for review.

A contraction is when two words are pushed together, and one or more letters gets popped out while an apostrophe gets pushed in.

Remember this?

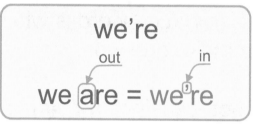

we're

out   in

we are = we're

out   in

you have ➡ you have   you've

 Read the words below.

you're	we've	don't	haven't
it's	they'll	doesn't	hasn't
I'm	he's	didn't	that's

Read the following sentences:

1. You've said that you couldn't say up late.
2. She's at the age where she wouldn't take a bath.
3. She'll see that you've studied for the test.
4. That's all of the food I'm going to bring to the party.
5. He doesn't want to go to bed early.

Exercise 34.1
Draw lines to match the contractions with their partners.

1. I'm   I have

2. I'll   have not

3. I've   they have

4. haven't   I am

5. they're   they are

6. they've   I will

7. he's   did not

8. didn't   he is

9. doesn't   she is

10. she's   does not

Contractions are touched on in this program, however, this concept
     may need more instruction and review outside of this book.

Exercise 34.2
Circle the contraction that makes sense.

1. <u>They're / They've</u> going to go to the grocery store later.

2. She <u>don't / doesn't</u> want to go home after class.

3. Do you think <u>she'll / she's</u> happy with her new pet?

4. <u>I've / I'm</u> going to go to the diner for dinner.

5. They <u>wasn't / weren't</u> going to stay for the weekend.

Exercise 34.3
Read the sentences and pick the two words that make sense and write the **contracted** form of those words on the line.

1. The baby _____*wouldn't*_____ eat the boiled chicken.
   (would not)   they are

2. I want to find out what _____ looking at.
   they are   did not

3. _____ been up all night with the kitten.
   Did not   We have

4. I _____ seen the car keys.
   did not   have not

5. You _____ talk in class.
   should not   they are

6. _____ going to go out later.
   We have   We are

Exercise 34.4

Complete the words with FLOSS words that make sense.

1. Dogs like to sn __ __ __ other dogs.

2. To get service, you must ring the b __ __ __ .

3. When fixing a cavity, the dentist may use a dr __ __ __ .

4. If you go away, I will m __ __ __ you.

5. To do something perfectly requires a lot of sk __ __ __ .

6. The opposite of "more" is l __ __ __ .

7. The child sp __ __ __ __ __ his milk on the floor.

8. I had too much st __ __ __ in my suitcase.

9. The boy would not swallow the p __ __ __ .

10. If you eat too much, you will get f __ __ __ .

Assign the dictations for this lesson,
and have your student play the on-line games below for this
lesson as well as prior lessons that need review.

Blast Off
Matching Game

Save the Earth
Reading Game

Lesson 35

Homophones

1) Review the flash cards.
2) Check the dictations from the previous lesson.

Homophones are words that sound the same
but have a different meaning.
Note that they *may or may not* be spelled the same.

 Read the homophones below.

sea - see	which - witch	would - wood
hi - high	here - hear	it's - its
blue - blew	maid - made	one - won

 There are many homophones,
and only a few are listed above.

Exercise 35.1
Circle the **homophone pairs** in the sentences below.
Note, there is **one** set of homophones in each sentence.

1. I won just one race at the picnic last summer.

2. The whole pool liner was replaced because of one hole.

3. I hear the music only when I'm here, next to the speaker.

4. The perfume that she sent to me had a nice scent.

5. In the morning, the maid made the bed.

6. The two girls ate too much ice-cream for dessert.

their → ownership
there → a place
they're → "they are"

Exercise 35.2

Circle the correct homophone in the sentences below.

their   there   they're

1. <u>Their / They're</u> going to catch the morning train.

2. They carried <u>their / there</u> suitcases to the hotel room.

3. I kept <u>their / there</u> cell phones in my bag.

4. I wanted to go <u>their / there</u> , to the zoo, after lunch.

5. <u>Their / There</u> are three things you should do first.

6. Why are <u>their / there</u> no more shirts for sale?

7. I think <u>there / they're</u> waiting for it to rain first.

8. <u>Their / There</u> dog jumped up onto my lap.

9. I always wanted to go over <u>there / they're</u>.

10. What time do they get <u>their / there</u> dinner?

What word do you see in all of the homophones below?
Underline this word.

their   there   they're

- 183 -

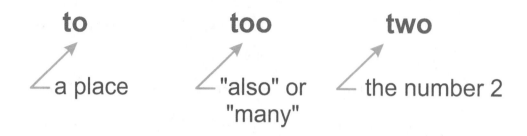

to → a place

too → "also" or "many"

two → the number 2

Exercise 35.3
Circle the correct homophone in the sentences below.

to   too   two

1. I wanted to / two / too   go home after school.

2. I like that song to / two / too .

3. Jon had to / two / too many things to / two / too do.

4. On Saturday, the baby turned to / two / too years old.

5. Let's see who will go to / two / too the lake with us.

Exercise 35.4
Circle the words that complete the sentences.

1. In September, I will be in fourth / forth grade.

2. The bloodhound picked up the man's cent / scent .

3. She scent / sent the letter in the mail / male .

4. A girl is a female, and a boy is a mail / male .

5. Jon ran the race and one / won .

Exercise 35.5
Circle the correct word that corresponds to the given meaning.

1. When two things come together.	meet / meat
2. To purchase something.	bye / buy / by
3. Opposite of rich.	pore / poor / pour
4. Something you do with your eyes.	sea / see
5. Something you do with your ears.	here / hear
6. One penny is a __?__.	cent / sent
7. First, second, third, __?__.	forth / fourth
8. The past tense of "throw".	through / threw

Exercise 35.6
Review: write the contraction for the words below.

1. can not _____

2. do not _____

3. it is _____

4. she will _____

5. she is _____

Homophones may or may not be recognized, by your students. It will depend on their prior instruction. This program introduces homophones, however, more instruction in this area may be needed.

Exercise 35.7
Add 'er' to the following words.

+ er

1. run   _____

2. easy   _____

3. cold   _____

4. wet   _____

5. happy _____

6. nice   _____

7. fat   _____

8. thin   _____

Assign the dictations for this lesson, and have your student play the on-line games for review.

1) Review the flash cards.
2) Check the dictations from the previous lesson.

There are many words that start with a 'wh'. Usually we say the following words with the /w/ sound, however, 'wh' is supposed to be a /w/ with air passing through.

wh   <u>wh</u>at   <u>wh</u>en   <u>wh</u>ere   <u>wh</u>y

Read the words below.

which	wheel	whack	whimper
while	white	whine	whisk
whale	whether	whisper	whisker

Exercise 36.1
Circle the words that make sense in the sentences below.

1. The dog <u>whined / wind</u> when he wanted to go outside.

2. The car turned right as I moved the steering <u>wheel / well</u>.

3. It took a while, then his cry faded to a <u>whisper / whimper</u>.

4. In a library, you should talk in a soft <u>whine / whisper.</u>

5. The white <u>wheel / whale</u> can be found in the Artic.

Words With Silent Letters

There are many words that contain letters that you don't hear.
Most of these silent letters are listed below.

> ### Common Silent Letters
> w h s n b k g/gh

wrist	island	doubt	gnaw
hour	autumn	knee	straight

 Read the words below.

answer	honor	column	known
toward	rhyme	climb	knife
wrinkle	debris	crumb	gnarl

Exercise 36.2
Circle the **silent letters** in the words below.

1. knee

2. knit

3. thumb

4. lamb

5. comb

6. knife

7. bomb

8. island

Exercise 36.3
Circle the word that matches the meaning.

1.	The opposite of day.	knight / night
2.	Use a pencil to do this.	write / right
3.	Having to do with seeing.	sight / site
4.	The opposite of "yes".	know / no
5.	The opposite of "low"	high / hi
6.	Sixty minutes.	hour / our
7.	The past tense of "old".	knew / new
8.	Means the entire thing.	whole / hole

Exercise 36.4
Circle the **silent letters** in the words below.

1. knight   4. autumn

2. two **2**   5. wrong

3. sword   6. write

Exercise 36.5
Fill in the missing letters for the words below.

h   k   n   w

1. g___ost

4. autum___

7. w___istle

2. w___ale

5. s___ord

8. ___rong

3. ___night

6. t___o **2**

9. ___rite

Exercise 36.6
Complete the words in the sentences below.

1. When you are very cold, your hands might get num____.

2. When you go to school, you learn to ____rite.

3. The coach blew his ___ ___ istle to start the race.

4. To open the door, turn the ____nob.

5. After summer comes autum____.

Assign the dictations for this lesson,
and have your student play the on-line games for review.

Words with Silent Letters - Reference

Silent 'b':

debt	dumb	plumber	climb
doubt	numb	tomb	bomb
crumb	thumb	lamb	comb

Silent 'g':

gnaw	gnash	foreign	design
gnat	gnarl	feign	reign
gnome	campaign	sign	align

straight   through = /throo/   thorough = /thuro/

Silent 'h':

hour	honor	heir	rhyme
herb	honest	ghost	rhythm

Silent 'k':

knee	knew	knife	knit
kneel	known	knight	knob
know	knuckle	knot	knock

Silent 'n':

autumn	column	condemn	hymn	solemn

Silent 's':

island	aisle	debris	Arkansas	Illinois

Silent 'w':

answer	two	wrap	whom	who
sword	write	wrong	whole	wrist
toward	wrote	wreck	whose	wrinkle

1) Review the flash cards.

2) Check the dictations from the previous lesson.

The next two lessons cover double vowel rule breakers, which show how we have words that do not follow the vowel team rule (where the first vowel does the talking). If your student does not have the common vowel teams mastered, then you should work on them before proceeding with this lesson.

Rule Breakers

Remember our common long vowel teams?

Now we have the rule breakers!

Here, the first vowel does NOT do the talking.

long 'a'

 ei — long 'a'

w<u>ei</u>gh   <u>ei</u>ght   n<u>ei</u>ghbor   v<u>ei</u>n

long 'e'

 ie — long 'e'

f<u>ie</u>ld   br<u>ie</u>f   p<u>ie</u>ce   cook<u>ie</u>

Read the words below.

chief	brownie	freight	island
grief	birdie	sleigh	column
belief	calorie	weight	autumn
believe	bootie	weighing	climb

message	bandage	average	notice	office

Exercise 37.1
Fill in the blanks to complete the words.

1. ch___ ___f

2. c___ ___k___ ___

3. gen___ ___

4. mov___ ___

5. hood___ ___

6. d___ gg___ ___

7. ___ ___ght

8. br___ ___n___ ___

9. b___ ___t___ ___

10. b___ ___d___ ___

Exercise 37.2
Read each sentence, and circle the words that make sense.

1. I don't believe / belief in ghosts.

2. It was a relieve / relief when I found my lost puppy.

3. The boys ran out onto the baseball field / piece.

4. Cut the cake into eight cookies / pieces.

5. Every morning the freight / fight train passes by.

6. The brownie / genie granted the man three wishes.

Exercise 37.3
Complete the sentences with the words that make sense.

brief   achieve   weight   neighbor   eight

1. I ate too much and gained _____.

2. The rain lasted for a _____ time.

3. When I was _____ years old, I was in third grade.

4. I would like to _____ my goals for today.

5. My _____ has a large pool.

Exercise 37.4

Read the words to your student, and have him/her circle the correct spelling for each word.

1.	free	frea	7.	brief	breaf
2.	seen	sean	8.	cooky	cookie
3.	feeld	field	9.	releef	relief
4.	eight	aight	10.	keep	keap
5.	fight	fite	11.	beleef	belief
6.	naybor	neighbor	12.	receeve	receive

Exercise 37.5

Write the sound that the underlined letter(s) make.

1. ri<u>gh</u>t	long ___		5. br<u>ie</u>f	long ___
2. tr<u>ay</u>	long ___		6. tr<u>y</u>	long ___
3. h<u>igh</u>	long ___		7. str<u>ay</u>	long ___
4. w<u>eigh</u>	long ___		8. ser<u>ie</u>s	long ___

Assign the dictations for this lesson,
and have your student play the on-line games for review.

1) Review the flash cards.
2) Check the dictations from the previous lesson.

Rule Breakers

Short 'e'

 short 'e'

br<u>ea</u>th   spr<u>ea</u>d   f<u>ea</u>ther   r<u>ea</u>dy

 Read the words below.

head	heavy	sweat	health
dead	steady	threat	weather
thread	already	deaf	dread

treasure*   measure*

* Note that 'sure' = /shur/. This will be covered in a later lesson.

Exercise 38.1

Complete the words below. Use 'ea' for the short 'e' sound.

1. m__ __sure

2. tr__ __sure

3. f__ __ __ __ers

4. h__ __vy

5. h__ __v__ __

6. sw__ __t__ __

Exercise 38.2

Read the words out loud and draw lines to match the words to their pictures.

1. head

2. bread

3. weapon

4. wealthy

5. weather

6. heavy

7. heaven

8. thread

9. measure

10. sweater

8 words where 'ea' has a long 'a'

Long 'a'

long 'a'

br<u>ea</u>k   b<u>ea</u>r   t<u>ea</u>r   sw<u>ea</u>r

st<u>ea</u>k   p<u>ea</u>r   w<u>ea</u>r   gr<u>ea</u>t

*In these <u>eight</u> words, it's the **second** vowel that does the talking.*

Exercise 38.3

Complete the words below. Use 'ea' for the long 'a' sound.

1.

p__ __ __

3.

b__ __ __

2.

st__ __ __

4.

t__ __ __

'ea' Review

'ea' can be a **long 'e'**, as in: b<u>ea</u>ch

'ea' can be a **short 'e'**, as in: br<u>ea</u>d

Only for **8** words.

'ea' can be a **long 'a'**, as in: p<u>ea</u>r

'ai' as a short 'e'

Short 'e'   short 'e'

ai

ag**ai**n	s**ai**d	cert**ai**n	fount**ai**n	capt**ai**n
ag**ai**nst	barg**ai**n	curt**ai**n	mount**ai**n	Brit**ai**n

This is not common and most of the words where 'ai' = short 'e' are listed above.

Exercise 38.4

Read the sentences and circle the words that are correctly spelled.

1. Jane _said / sed_ that I could go with her.

2. Jim leaned _agenst / against_ the wall.

3. We planned on climbing the _mountain / mounten_.

4. We were _certen / certain_ that he wasn't home.

5. I wish I could see you _agen / again_, before I go.

'ai' Review

'ai' can be a **long 'a'**, as in: p**ai**l

'ai' can be a **short 'e'**, as in: fount**ai**n

Exercise 38.5
Draw lines to match the rhyming words.

1. head   foam

2. eight   spite

3. limb   fine

4. sign   sealed

5. comb   him

6. right   leaf

7. field   bed

8. grief   state

Exercise 38.6
For each line below, circle the two words that rhyme.

1.   said   bread   paid

2.   seat   great   plate

3.   right   eight   late

4.   sweeter   sweater   wetter

5.   leather   leader   weather

Assign the dictations for this lesson,
and have your student play the on-line games for review.

1) Review the flash cards.
2) Check the dictations from the previous lesson.

'tial' & 'cial' make the /shull/ sound.
* or /shuhl/

/shull/

tial

/shull/

par<u>tial</u> mar<u>tial</u> substan<u>tial</u>
essen<u>tial</u> creden<u>tial</u> confiden<u>tial</u>

/shull/

cial

/shull/

spe<u>cial</u> cru<u>cial</u> commer<u>cial</u>

/ishull/

icial

short 'i'

artif<u>icial</u> off<u>icial</u> benef<u>icial</u>

Read the words below.

official	crucial	sweet	great
initial	social	sweat	avoid
special	gigantic	success	simplify
partial	dangerous	toward	answer

Read the following sentences:
1. The commercial on TV was for toothpaste.
2. It was official, the wedding would be in September.
3. The puppy was very social.
4. I especially liked the chocolate fudge ice-cream.
5. The trip to the museum was special.

Exercise 39.1
Circle the words that make sense for the sentences below.

1. It is official / crucial that you see a doctor.

2. My surprise birthday party was very special / presidential.

3. The document was marked confidential / initial.

4. We initially / socially wanted to leave early.

5. She had mud on her face for a facial / financial.

6. I live in a residential / superficial neighborhood.

Exercise 39.2
Circle the words that have the long 'e' sound (hint: there are 3).

tied	cookie	bear	eight
field	captain	great	movie

Exercise 39.3
Circle the sound for the letters that are underlined.

1. br<u>ie</u>f   long 'e'   long 'i'
2. f<u>ie</u>ld   long 'e'   long 'i'
3. br<u>ea</u>th   long 'e'   short 'e'
4. br<u>ea</u>the   long 'e'   short 'e'
5. beh<u>i</u>nd   long 'i'   short 'i'
6. s<u>ai</u>d   long 'a'   short 'e'
7. gr<u>ea</u>t   long 'a'   long 'e'
8. cert<u>ai</u>n   long 'a'   short 'e'

Exercise 39.4
Draw lines to match the rhyming words.

1. climb   gum
2. numb   bite
3. known   spout
4. which   led
5. tight   pitch
6. head   chime
7. doubt   groan

Exercise 39.5
Complete the crossword puzzle.

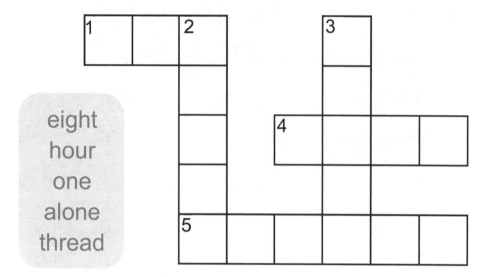

eight
hour
one
alone
thread

Across

1. The number before two.

4. Sixty minutes makes an___.

5. To sew, you need a needle and ___.

Down

2. The number that comes before nine.

3. When you are all by yourself, you are ___.

Assign the dictations for this lesson,
and have your student play the on-line games for review.

1) Review the flash cards.
2) Check the dictations from the previous lesson.

'tion' & 'sion' = /shun/

tion fric<u>tion</u>   construc<u>tion</u>   por<u>tion</u>

sion ses<u>sion</u>   permis<u>sion</u>   discus<u>sion</u>

'tion' & 'sion' **after** a vowel

* All beginning vowels are long, except the 'i'.

'sion' = /zshun/

ation		asion	
etion	n<u>ation</u>	esion	inv<u>asion</u>
<u>i</u>tion	comple<u>tion</u>	<u>i</u>sion	<u>l</u>esion
	defin<u>ition</u>		v<u>ision</u>
otion	m<u>otion</u>	osion	expl<u>osion</u>
ution	sol<u>ution</u>	usion	ill<u>usion</u>

For words that are complex, block out parts of the word, showing only sounds that your student knows, one at a time. This will help in decoding larger words, by training your student to look for familiar sounds.

Read the words below.

action	illusion	decision	corrosion
option	caution	division	edition
mission	motion	confusion	solution

Read the following sentences:

1. We will go to New York City for vacation.
2. The definition was in the dictionary.
3. Jade won a prize in the spelling competition.
4. The celebration was for the promotion.
5. The director shouted, "Action!"

Exercise 40.1
Draw lines to match the words to their correct math equation.

1. addition   3 x 4 = 12

2. subtraction   2 + 1 = 3

3. multiplication   8 ÷ 4 = 2

4. division   5 - 4 = 1

Exercise 40.2
Complete the sentences with the words that make sense.

lotion   mission   caution   transportation   solution

1. The team of astronauts were on a _____ to land on the moon.

2. People use _____ on their dry skin.

3. Planes, trains and automobiles are forms

   of _____.

4. Our teacher wanted to know the _____ to the problem.

5. You must use _____ when walking on ice.

Exercise 40.3
Circle the sound that the underlined letters make.

1. gr<u>ea</u>t	long 'e'	long 'a'
2. m<u>igh</u>t	long 'i'	long 'a'
3. w<u>ei</u>ght	long 'e'	long 'a'
4. <u>ei</u>ght	long 'e'	long 'a'
5. br<u>ie</u>f	long 'e'	long 'i'
6. f<u>ie</u>ld	long 'e'	long 'i'

Exercise 40.4
Read the sentences and circle the correct words.

1. To find the meaning of a word, you use a <u>?</u>.

   mission   dictionary

2. The number of people that live in a certain place.

   creation   population

3. A person who is an expert in his or her work.

   professional   tension

4. The meaning of a certain word.

   passion   definition

5. A connection that a person has to another person.

   nation   relationship

Exercise 40.5
Circle the words that makes sense for the sentences below.

1. The old car was in good condition / transition.

2. My special catcher's mitt was swimming / missing.

3. The dancer went to submission / audition for the show.

4. Believe it or not, he was telling the truth / bathtub.

5. We play soccer on a pillow / field.

6. He likes to eat bread / kittens with peanut butter.

Exercise 40.6

Circle the words that makes sense for the sentences below. Be careful, the words are homophones, and you may need help.

1. I need a new pair / pear of sneakers.

2. I like bananas, apples, and pairs / pears.

3. For dinner, I will order stake / steak.

4. We use a stake / steak to fix the tent to the ground.

5. Please grate / great the cheese for the salad.

6. You did a great / grate job on your project.

Exercise 40.7

Circle the sound that the underlined letters make.

1. f<u>igh</u>t	long 'i'	long 'a'
2. r<u>ea</u>dy	long 'e'	short 'e'
3. inst<u>ea</u>d	long 'e'	short 'e'
4. rel<u>ie</u>f	long 'e'	long 'i'
5. n<u>eigh</u>bor	long 'e'	long 'a'

Assign the dictations for this lesson.
Note that these words are longer and
more difficult. You may want your student
to study the words first. *Also, encourage
your student to use the phonics chart on the
back cover of this book to help spell words.*

Review
Lessons 31-40

1) Review the flash cards.
2) Check the dictations from the previous lesson.

 Read the words below.

families	scroll	numb	weight	special
bushes	most	know	breath	vacation
control	who	island	certain	occasion
scold	doesn't	believe	partial	vision

Exercise R4.1
Circle the words that are correctly spelled.

1.	answer	anser	5.	rong	wrong
2.	dout	doubt	6.	clime	climb
3.	thum	thumb	7.	island	iland
4.	toward	toard	8.	crum	crumb

Exercise R4.2
Write the **plural** form of the words below.

1. batch   _____

2. wish   _____

3. box   _____

4. city   _____

5. knife   _____

Exercise R4.3
Complete the sentences below with the words that make sense.

knot   knife   knee   answer   knob   know

1. Your leg bends at the _____ .

2. What is the _____ to the question?

3. It is nice to _____ a lot about a subject.

4. To cut the meat you'll need a _____ .

5. His shoe laces were tied in a _____ .

6. Turn the door- _____ to open the door.

Exercise R4.4
Circle the words that are correctly spelled.

1. ate / eight

2. cookie / cooky

3. bread / bred

4. pair / pear

5. swetter / sweater

6. head / hed

7. bear / bair

8. welthy / wealthy

Exercise R4.5
Complete the sentences below with the words that make sense.

| healthy | vision | nutrition | measure | wealthy |

1. Bad eye-sight means poor _____ .

2. You may use a ruler to _____ something.

3. If you're not sick, then you are _____ .

4. If you have a lot of money, you are _____ .

5. You must eat proper food for good _____ .

Exercise R4.6
Draw lines to match the words to their contractions.

1. I will		they'll
2. I am		we've
3. they are		I'll
4. they will		it'll
5. it is		they're
6. it will		it's
7. we have		we're
8. we are		I'm

Exercise R4.7
Circle the **five** words where **'ea'** has the **short 'e'** sound.

meat   heat   bear   health

head   feather   dear   beach

great   heavy   ready   real

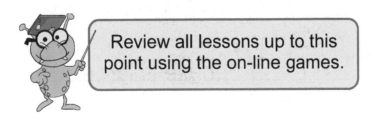

Review all lessons up to this point using the on-line games.

Apostrophes for Ownership

When a noun **owns** something, an apostrophe 's' or an 's' *followed* by an apostrophe must be added.

Rules for Apostrophes & Ownership

1. If there is one owner, add an apostrophe and then the 's'.

2. If there is *more than one owner,* add the 's' and **then** the apostrophe.

The dog house is owned by **one** dog.

Put apostrophe *before* the 's'.

The dog's house is small.

The dog house is owned by **more than one** dog.

Put apostrophe *after* the 's'.

The dogs' house is large.

The word "its" is the *exception* to the ownership rule!

The apostrophe in "it's" is **not** for ownership;
it is a contraction for "it is".

$\times$ The dog wagged <u>it's</u> tail.

$\checkmark$ The dog wagged <u>its</u> tail.

Exercise 41.1
Circle the words that have apostrophes for ownership.

* Be careful, not all apostrophes are for ownership!

1. I doubt my grandfather's vision is good.

2. The baby's crib is purple.

3. They're looking at Jim's new bicycle.

4. It's interesting how the bird's feathers are so bright.

5. My father's car was in a collision.

6. Where did you go with Sam's bicycle?

7. We're going to go to Emily's house.

8. The dogs' dishes were empty.

Exercise 41.2
Add apostrophes for ownership; some words may need an apostrophe and some may not.

1. My <u>dogs</u> hair is brown.

2. My three <u>dogs</u> all like to eat meat.

3. <u>Johns</u> house is just around the corner.

4. The teacher collected the <u>students</u> papers.

5. <u>Jills</u> bicycle was leaning against the house.

Exercise 41.3
Circle the correct words for the sentences below.

1. She likes the fact that <u>its / it's</u> Friday.

2. After lunch, <u>their / they're</u> going to the library.

3. We <u>were / we're</u> looking for a nice place for our vacation.

4. What do you think of <u>there / their</u> new puppy?

5. What is Frank going to do when he gets <u>there / their</u> ?

6. <u>Were / We're</u> you at the store earlier today?

Exercise 41.4

Circle the sounds on the right that match the sounds on the left. There is one match per line.

1.	tion	igh	sion	tial
2.	oy	oo	ou	oi
3.	ew	oi	oo	ou
4.	cial	tial	tion	ew
5.	oa	ew	au	ow
6.	ee	ea	ew	ai
7.	ai	oi	ay	ie
8.	ie	igh	ow	ue
9.	er	or	ar	ur
10.	aw	er	au	ow

Exercise 41.5

Complete the words in the sentences below.

1. On the boat, I got m_o_ t _i_ _o_ _n_ sickness.

2. I tried to answer the ques___ ___ ___ ___.

3. There was a big birthday celebr___ ___ ___ ___ ___.

4. I had to find the defin___ ___ ___ ___ ___ for the word.

5. She went to the hospital for an oper___ ___ ___ ___ ___.

Exercise 41.6
Write the words, with apostrophes for ownership, on the lines.

1. _____ puppy was very excited to see me.
   Jade

2. _____ turtle likes to watch television.
   Amy

3. The girls went to _____ house after school.
   Joey

4. I borrowed _____ pencil.
   Mary

5. My _____ classroom was decorated nicely.
   teacher

6. The _____ bathroom is down the hallway.
   boys (more than one)

Exercise 41.7
Circle the **four** words that have the **long 'a'** sound.

weight	raining	tank
mountain	again	fountain
curtain	braid	bargain

Have your student play the on-line games for review.
This lesson does **not** have dictations. Instead, have your
student review dictations that were problematic.

> 1) Review the flash cards.
> 2) Check the dictations from the previous lesson.

words ending with **'o'**	long 'o'
	hell<u>o</u> als<u>o</u> zer<u>o</u> tomat<u>o</u>

words ending with **'a'**	/uh/
	sof<u>a</u> comm<u>a</u> dat<u>a</u> Florid<u>a</u>

i ➡ long 'e'

In words that end with vowels,
usually 'i' sounds like long 'e'.

words ending with **'i'**	long 'e'
	tax<u>i</u> sk<u>i</u> graffit<u>i</u> confett<u>i</u>

words ending with **'ia'**	long 'e' then /uh/
	med<u>ia</u> bacter<u>ia</u> hyster<u>ia</u> Ind<u>ia</u>

words ending with **'io'**	long 'e' then long 'o'
	rad<u>io</u> pat<u>io</u> stud<u>io</u> aud<u>io</u>

Words ending with 'u' are not discussed since it is uncommon. You may want to tell your student that words that end with 'u' end with either long 'u' or /oo/, such as "menu" and "snafu".

 Read the words below.

solo	Alaska	confetti	Columbia	radio
auto	America	taxi	hysteria	scorpio
buffalo	salsa	chili	mania	studio
potato	arena	mini	India	cheerio

Exercise 42.1
Circle the sounds on the right that match the <u>underlined</u> letters on the left.

1. pota<u>to</u>	long 'o'	/uh/	'e'-'o'
2. extr<u>a</u>	long 'o'	/uh/	'e'-'o'
3. rad<u>io</u>	long 'o'	/uh/	'e'-'o'
4. stud<u>io</u>	long 'o'	/uh/	'e'-'o'
5. zebr<u>a</u>	long 'o'	/uh/	'e'-'o'
6. zer<u>o</u>	long 'o'	/uh/	'e'-'o'
7. als<u>o</u>	long 'o'	/uh/	'e'-'o'
8. dat<u>a</u>	long 'o'	/uh/	'e'-'o'

Exercise 42.2
Complete the sentences with the words that make sense.

| family | America | tornado | bacteria | tomato |

1. Seek shelter if a _____ is near.

2. An infection can be caused by a _____.

3. I planted _____ plants in my garden.

4. The large _____ needs a mini-van.

5. The president of _____ can veto a bill.

Exercise 42.3
Circle the words that make sense for the sentences below.

1. For lunch we'll have tuna / tuba fish sandwiches.

2. Let's take a ride in the pasta / taxi.

3. Last winter it got below zero / mini degrees.

4. We listened to the music on the pizza / radio.

5. Put your feet up on the sofa / piano and relax!

6. Use a comma / coma to separate words in a list.

7. Our teacher gave us soda / extra homework.

Exercise 42.4
Complete the words for the pictures below.

1. z _ _ _ _ _

2. _ _ z z _

3. t _ _ _ _

4. r _ _ _ _ _

5. t _ _ _ _

6. p _ _ _ _ _

7. p _ _ _ _ _

8. t _ _ _ _ _

In many words, 'i' can be a long 'e'.

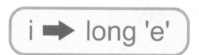

material	memorial
medium	stadium
librarian	Canadian
experience	audience
ingredient	orient

Exercise 42.5
Circle the words that make sense in the sentences below.

1. The <u>sodium / helium</u> balloon floated into the air.

2. The boy would not eat the <u>ingredient / broccoli.</u>

3. A sentence usually ends with a <u>librarian / period</u>.

4. Jim ordered a <u>medium / helium</u> sized soda.

5. I have a lot of <u>experience / material</u> in gymnastics.

6. I needed to purchase a <u>stadium / medium</u> sized shirt.

7. She wouldn't reveal her secret <u>ingredient / librarian</u>.

8. He stuffed the tomato and lettuce into the <u>patio / pita</u>.

9. We went to the <u>stadium / broccoli</u> to see the game.

10. A person who studies history is a <u>historian / hysterical</u>.

Assign the dictations for this lesson, and have your student play the on-line games for review.

1) Review the flash cards.
2) Check the dictations from the previous lesson.

'le' has the /l/ sound.

le

samp<u>le</u>	ank<u>le</u>	eag<u>le</u>
artic<u>le</u>	ang<u>le</u>	dood<u>le</u>

Read the words below.

mingle	candle	dimple	simple
jingle	double	gentle	marble
jiggle	trouble	gurgle	mumble
cargo	antenna	insomnia	official
ego	area	pizzeria	social
logo	umbrella	bacteria	crucial

Exercise 43.1
Complete the words below; all words end with 'le'.

1.  c _ _ _ _ _

3. a _ _ _ _ _

2. h _ _ _ _ _

4.  t _ _ _ _ _

⭐ 'le' acts like **one** letter - an 'e', but with a /l/ sound. ⭐

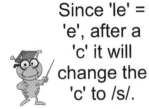

Since 'le' = 'e', after a 'c' it will change the 'c' to /s/.

e
muscle
⎵
— /s/

e
maple
⎵
— long 'a'

Since 'le' = 'e', it can change a short vowel to a long vowel.

Since 'le' acts like an 'e', a consonant must be **doubled to protect a short vowel.**

li**tt**le   ri**pp**le   ri**dd**le

Exercise 43.2
Complete the words below.

Remember to protect your short vowels.

1. k __ __ __ __ __

4. b __ __ __ __ __

2. a __ __ __ __

5. b __ __ __ __ __

3. p__ __ __ __ __

6. w__ __ __ __ __

 Point out how all of the words above have short vowels that need to be protected from the 'le', which acts like an 'e'.

Also, point out how in #6, the word "waffle" has an 'a' that sounds like a short 'o'.

able
ible

'a' = long 'a', or
'a' = /uh/

the 'i' is short

st<u>able</u>   cur<u>able</u>   divis<u>ible</u>

c<u>able</u>   detect<u>able</u>   invis<u>ible</u>

 Read the words below.

table	acceptable	horrible	incredible
fable	portable	edible	flexible
notable	collectable	possible	terrible

Exercise 43.3
Circle the words that make sense in the sentences below.

1. He was not able to jump over the <u>riddle / puddle</u>.

2. The rotten <u>apple / puzzle</u> was not edible.

3. The baby wanted the <u>kettle / bottle</u> of milk.

4. Hold the pitcher by its <u>middle / handle</u>.

5. The puppy likes to <u>cuddle / battle</u> with the boy.

6. The horrible disease was not <u>invisible / curable</u>.

7. The gymnast was very <u>flexible / notable</u>.

Exercise 43.4
Complete the sentences with the words that make sense.

> visible   ankle   stable   possible   noodles

1. Cook the _____ in boiling water.

2. The horse stays in the _____ .

3. At nighttime, the sun is not _____ .

4. The skater tripped and broke her _____ .

5. It is not _____ to touch your elbow to your chin.

Exercise 43.5
Write the sound that the underlined letter(s) make.

1. bel<u>ie</u>ve	long ____		5. mount<u>ai</u>n	short ____
2. gr<u>ea</u>t	long ____		6. br<u>ea</u>d	short ____
3. fl<u>igh</u>t	long ____		7. capt<u>ai</u>n	short ____
4. b<u>ea</u>r	long ____		8. pos<u>i</u>tion	short ____

> Assign the dictations for this lesson,
> and have your student play the on-line games for review.

Lesson 44 — Words Ending with 'ture' and 'sure'

1) Review the flash cards.
2) Check the dictations from the previous lesson.

'ture' = /chur/

/chur/

ture

fu<u>ture</u>   mois<u>ture</u>   furni<u>ture</u>

Read the words below.

feature	picture	nature	culture
fracture	mixture	mature	lecture

Exercise 44.1

Circle the words that make sense in the sentences below.

1. The picture hung on the wall in the <u>hallway / pool</u>.

2. Put your signature on the bottom of the <u>shark / paper</u>.

3. Can a crystal ball be used to see the <u>future / tornado</u>?

4. On nature walks, one can see many <u>lampshades / birds</u>.

5. We played Capture the Flag in <u>gym / potato</u> class.

6. Stand up straight for good <u>structure / posture</u>.

7. The trip was quite an <u>adventure / expenditure</u>.

/shur/

'sure' = /shur/

sure

pres<u>sure</u>   plea<u>sure</u>   clo<u>sure</u>

 Read the words below.

| assure | unsure | treasure |
| exposure | leisure | measure |

Exercise 44.2

Circle the sounds on the right that match the sounds on the left. There is only one per line.

1.	ture	/shun/	/chur/	long 'u'
2.	tion	/shur/	/shun/	/chur/
3.	sure	/shull/	/shun/	/shur/
4.	igh	long 'a'	long 'i'	/j/
5.	ay	long 'a'	/ou/	long 'e'
6.	tial	/shun/	long 'i'	/shull/
7.	cial	/shun/	long 'i'	/shull/
8.	sion	/shun/	/oy/	/shur/

Exercise 44.3
Circle the words that make sense in the sentences below.

1. A mixture / pressure of sugar water can make candy.

2. The sheep were out in the picture / pasture.

3. The texture / temperature is ninety degrees.

4. The boy fell and fractured / measured his arm.

5. Tom measured / punctured the balloon with a needle.

6. In the nature / future , you should check the weather.

Exercise 44.4
Circle the answers to the questions below.

1. When 'c' is followed by 'e', 'i', or 'y', it always / sometimes has the /s/ sound.

2. When 'g' is followed by 'e', 'i', or 'y', it always / sometimes has the /j/ sound.

3. Often, an 'i' can have the long 'a' / long 'e' sound.

4. When 'y' is in the **middle** of a word, it can have the long or short 'e' sound / 'i' sound.

5. Can a word **end** with the letter 'j'? yes / no

Exercise 44.5
Write the words below in their **plural** form.

1. story   _____

2. lady   _____

3. party   _____

4. baby   _____

5. * ability   _____

6. * body   _____

7. memory   _____

8. dictionary   _____

* Many longer words, more than one syllable,
often do not follow the **V**C**V** long vowel rule.
We can see this in the two words below.

short 'i'   short 'o'

ability   body

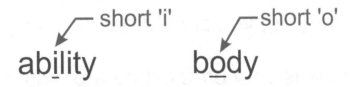

Assign the dictations for this lesson,
and have your student play the on-line games for review.

Lesson 45 — Words Ending with 'ous' and 'ious'

1) Review the flash cards.
2) Check the dictations from the previous lesson.

'ous' = /us/

/us/

ous

/us/

danger<u>ous</u>   nerv<u>ous</u>   glamor<u>ous</u>

'ious' *sometimes* = 'e' - /us/

'e' - /us/

ious

'i' = long 'e'

prev<u>ious</u>   ser<u>ious</u>   hilar<u>ious</u>

 Point out that here is an example of when 'i' acts like a long 'e'.

Exercise 45.1
Circle the words that make sense in the sentences below.

1. If you are very well known, you are <u>famous / serious</u>.

2. When studying, you should be <u>nervous / serious</u>.

3. If someone is very pretty, they are <u>famous / gorgeous</u>.

4. Monkeys are often described as <u>glamorous / curious</u>.

5. Walking in the middle of the road is <u>dangerous / famous</u>.

The /shus/ Sound

If 'ious' *follows* a 'c', 't' or 'x', then those letters combined with 'ious' sounds like /shus/.

/shus/

cious
tious
xious

/shus/

pre<u>cious</u>

gra<u>cious</u>

suspi<u>cious</u>

vi<u>cious</u>

cau<u>tious</u>

nutri<u>tious</u>

ambi<u>tious</u>

an<u>xious</u>

obno<u>xious</u>

Exercise 45.2

Circle the words that make sense in the sentences below.

1. The <u>precious / nutritious</u> gem stone sparkled.

2. The meal was very <u>nutritious / suspicious</u>.

3. The police officer said the boy was <u>suspicious / precious</u>.

4. Be <u>cautious / dangerous</u> when walking on ice.

5. People who worry a lot may be <u>suspicious / anxious</u>.

6. The <u>gracious / vicious</u> lie was spread around the town.

7. The host of the party was very <u>gracious / obnoxious</u>.

8. My little brother thinks he's funny, but he is really <u>anxious / obnoxious</u>

Exercise 45.3
Circle the sounds on the right that match the <u>underlined</u> letters on the left.

1. fam<u>ous</u>	/us/	/shus/	'e' - /us/
2. obv<u>ious</u>	/us/	/shus/	'e' - /us/
3. nerv<u>ous</u>	/us/	/shus/	'e' - /us/
4. gra<u>cious</u>	/us/	/shus/	'e' - /us/
5. cau<u>tious</u>	/us/	/shus/	'e' - /us/
6. danger<u>ous</u>	/us/	/shus/	'e' - /us/
7. ser<u>ious</u>	/us/	/shus/	'e' - /us/
8. suspi<u>cious</u>	/us/	/shus/	'e' - /us/

Exercise 45.4
Circle the words that make sense in the sentences.

1. If you are very angry, you are glamorous / furious.

2. The dancer practiced in the studio / radio.

3. The popular boy has numerous / obvious friends.

4. Too / Two and "also" mean the same thing.

5. The answer to the problem is obvious / dangerous.

Exercise 45.5
Circle the matching sounds, there is one per line.

1. ous	us	ou	oy
2. oi	'o'	oy	ou
3. tial	tale	shull	tile
4. tion	tial	cial	shun
5. cial	shull	us	shun
6. eigh	'a'	'e'	'i'
7. igh	'a'	'e'	'i'

Exercise 45.6
Add 'ing' to the following words and read them out loud.

+ ing

1. run _____

2. slip _____

3. carry _____

4. identify _____

5. shake _____

6. break _____

Exercise 45.7
Circle the meanings to the definitions listed.

1. Acting more than your age: mature / nutritious

2. The same: capture / equal

3. Tastes great: delicious / solution

4. Feeling sorry for: division / compassion

5. A very large house: mansion / envious

6. A different form of something: version / alter

7. Easy to see: curious / obvious

8. Many or a lot of: nervous / numerous

9. Harmful: dangerous / suspicious

10. To be extra careful: cautious / anxious

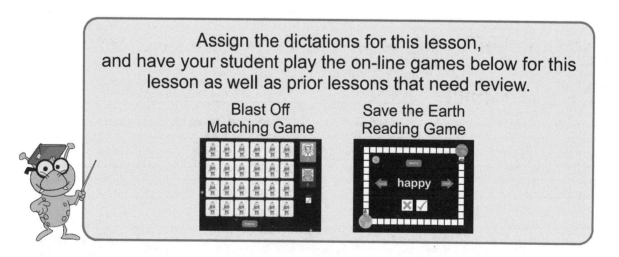

Assign the dictations for this lesson,
and have your student play the on-line games below for this
lesson as well as prior lessons that need review.

Blast Off
Matching Game

Save the Earth
Reading Game

happy

1) Review the flash cards.
2) Check the dictations from the previous lesson.

Remember how there are *no words* that **end** with a 'j'? There are also **no words that end with 'v'**.

 Words that end with /v/ end with 've'.

Since 'v' never gets doubled to protect a short vowel, the vowel **before** the 've' can be <u>long</u> or <u>short</u>.

— short 'i'

| live | massive | negative |
| give | positive | captive |

— long 'i'

| live | drive | five |
| survive | arrive | revive |

How do I know if the 'e' in 've' makes a nearby vowel long?

You don't. You have to try it both ways and see if it's a word you know and if it makes sense. See the sentence below.

Someday, I'd like to <u>live</u> near a <u>live</u> horse farm.

Why don't we double the
'v' to protect the short vowel?

The letter 'v' never gets doubled.

★ Remember: The following
consonants **cannot** be doubled:

c   h   j   k   q   v̲   w   x   y

Exercise 46.1

Circle the words that make sense in the sentences below.

1. The gold handbag was very <u>expensive / abusive</u>.

2. The opposite of positive is <u>inventive / negative</u>.

3. Her package will <u>survive / arrive</u> next Friday.

4. The boys were very <u>talkative / expensive</u>.

5. The movie star was very <u>relative / attractive</u>.

6. The artist is very <u>creative / aggressive</u>.

7. His puppies are very <u>negative / active</u>.

8. The holiday party is very <u>assertive / festive</u>.

Exercise 46.2
Circle the sounds that the underlined 'i's makes.

1.	str<u>i</u>ve	long 'i'	short 'i'
2.	dr<u>i</u>ve	long 'i'	short 'i'
3.	g<u>i</u>ve	long 'i'	short 'i'
4.	fest<u>i</u>ve	long 'i'	short 'i'
5.	surv<u>i</u>ve	long 'i'	short 'i'
6.	al<u>i</u>ve	long 'i'	short 'i'

Exercise 46.3
Answer the questions below.

1. For words that end with /v/, use ___ ___ for the /v/.

2. For words that end with /j/, use: ___ ___ for the /j/.

3. What letters after 'c' turns 'c' into /s/? ___ ___ ___

4. What letters after 'g' can turn 'g' into /j/? ___ ___ ___

In the words below, 'ove' = /uv/.

l<u>ove</u>   d<u>ove</u>   gl<u>ove</u>   ab<u>ove</u>   sh<u>ove</u>   sh<u>ove</u>l

Point out how the words above do not follow the long
vowel VCV rule, and the 'o' sounds like a short 'u'.
Also point out that "dove" could also have a long 'o', as
in: "She dove into the pool".

Exercise 46.4
Write the words for the pictures below.

1. _ _ _ _ _ _   _ _ _ _ _ _ _

2. _ _ _ _ _ _   _ _ _ _ _ _ _

3. _ _ _ _ _   _ _ _ _ _ _ _

4. _ _ _ _   _ _ _ _ _ _

Exercise 46.5
Circle the words that make sense in the sentences below.

1. We rearranged the _furnace / furniture_ in Justin's room.

2. I used _solution / lotion_ on my dry hands.

3. Driving in a snow storm is _cautious / dangerous_.

4. The baby was a nice _condition / addition_ to the family.

5. The _initial / special_ delivery arrived yesterday morning.

Assign the dictations for this lesson,
and have your student play the on-line games for review.

'ch' as /sh/ and /k/

1) Review the flash cards.
2) Check the dictations from the previous lesson.

In Lesson 5, we learned that 'ch' makes the /ch/ sound as in "chop". In this lesson, we will see how 'ch' also can have the /sh/ sound and the /k/ sound.

1	2	3
/ch/	/sh/	/k/

<u>'ch' as /sh/:</u> Usually when a word is "French" in nature.

machine   parachute   Chicago

<u>'ch' as /k/:</u> Usually when a word is "technical" in nature.

echo   technical   character

Read the following sentences:

1. The chef made a tasty bowl of mushroom soup.

2. The mechanic fixed the engine on the train.

3. A repetition of sound is called an echo.

4. My father has a mustache.

5. My friend lives in the city of Chicago.

6. The main character of the story was brave.

Exercise 47.1
Draw lines to match the words to their pictures.

1. para<u>ch</u>ute

2. <u>ch</u>andelier

3. ma<u>ch</u>ine

4. <u>ch</u>ef

5. stoma<u>ch</u>

6. <u>ch</u>emicals

7. musta<u>ch</u>e

8. <u>ch</u>ivalry

9. s<u>ch</u>ool

10. me<u>ch</u>anic

Exercise 47.2
Circle the words where 'ch' has the /k/ sound (there are 5).

ch = /k/

para<u>ch</u>ute   me<u>ch</u>anic   a<u>ch</u>e   <u>ch</u>aos

e<u>ch</u>o   s<u>ch</u>ool   <u>ch</u>arm   <u>ch</u>ampion

Exercise 47.3
Circle the words that make sense in the sentences below.

1. When I'm hungry, my stomach / machine may growl.

2. I woke up with a bad head- echo / ache.

3. The mechanic / character in the story was brave.

4. What chemicals / parachutes do they use to clean?

5. The hotel lobby had a large parachute / chandelier.

Exercise 47.4
Circle sound that the 'ch' makes in the words below.

1.	echo	/ch/ as in "chop"	/k/	/sh/
2.	school	/ch/ as in "chop"	/k/	/sh/
3.	chef	/ch/ as in "chop"	/k/	/sh/
4.	channel	/ch/ as in "chop"	/k/	/sh/
5.	chemist	/ch/ as in "chop"	/k/	/sh/
6.	Chicago	/ch/ as in "chop"	/k/	/sh/
7.	wrench	/ch/ as in "chop"	/k/	/sh/
8.	Michigan	/ch/ as in "chop"	/k/	/sh/
9.	chord	/ch/ as in "chop"	/k/	/sh/
10.	mechanic	/ch/ as in "chop"	/k/	/sh/

Exercise 47.5

For each sentence, complete the missing words with the sounds listed.

| ture | ation | tion | ive | ous | ach | atch | igh |

1. F i c _ _ _ _ _ _ means that the story isn't real.

2. The f a m _ _ _ _ actor stopped to pose for pictures.

3. We go to school to get an e d u c _ _ _ _ _ _ _.

4. If hungry, your s t o m _ _ _ may growl.

5. The dog used his leg to s c r _ _ _ _ _ his itch.

6. The sun was too b r _ _ _ _ _ t to look at.

7. I took a p i c _ _ _ _ _ of my best friend.

8. To stay healthy, you should keep a c t _ _ _ _.

Assign the dictations for this lesson,
and have your student play the on-line games for review.

1) Review the flash cards.
2) Check the dictations from the previous lesson.

'ph' *usually* has the /f/ sound.

/f/

ph

— /f/

phone   phrase   dolphin   sphere

Read the words below.

alphabet	elephant	nephew	pharmacist
autograph	graph	orphan	phone
dolphin	microphone	phantom	phonics

Exercise 48.1
Circle the words that make sense in the sentences below.

1. The dolphin / phone rang three times.

2. The globe has the shape of a elephant / sphere.

3. We saw the orphan / dolphin jump out of the water.

4. If you are in first place you may get a graphic / trophy.

5. The man on stage spoke into a microphone / phantom.

6. There are twenty-six letters in the trophy / alphabet.

'gh' is sometimes silent, but *sometimes* it has the /f/ sound.

/f/

| laugh | rough | enough |
| cough | tough | trough |

'gh' as /f/ is not very popular, and most of the words are listed above.

Exercise 48.2
Complete the sentences with the words that make sense.

| rough | laugh | tough |
| cough | enough | graph |

1. We had _____ cake to share with everyone.

2. In science class, we had to plot a _____ .

3. Sandpaper is not soft, it is very _____ .

4. The science test wasn't easy, it was _____ .

5. When Ethan got sick, he had a bad _____ .

6. The funny joke made me _____ .

'aught' & 'ought' both have the /awt/ sound

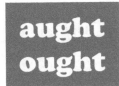

caught	sought
taught	fought
daughter	brought
slaughter	thought

Exercise 48.3
Complete the words using the given letters.

b   br   th   f

1. The two angry boys ____ought over the toy truck.

2. She ____ought she knew the answer.

3. I went to the store and ___ought a new dress.

4. He ___ought his little brother over to our house.

Exercise 48.4
Circle the words that make sense in the sentences below.

1. The lady's daughter came home from mars / school.

2. We were taught how to add and subtract / drive.

3. The past tense of "think" is thunk / thought.

4. Grandma bought / fought a new outfit at the store.

5. Ryan brought / bought his favorite movie to the party.

Exercise 48.5
Match the sounds below.

1. ph   /chur/

2. igh   /shur/

3. aught   /v/

4. sure   long 'i'

5. oi   /j/

6. ous   oy

7. ture   /us/

8. ve   /awt/

9. ge   /s/

10. ce   /f/

Assign the dictations for this lesson,
and have your student play the on-line games for review.

Words Ending with 'ician'

1) Review the flash cards.
2) Check the dictations from the previous lesson.

'ician' makes the /ĭshun/ sound.

short 'i'

/ishun/

ician

musician   magician
politician   technician
physician   dietician

This sound is usually at the **end** of a word.

magician

This ending usually has to do with an occupation.

Review - read the words below.

notice	taught	enough	mechanic
service	caught	tough	mechanical
practice	daughter	rough	chemical
office	bought	laugh	chemist
necklace	brought	laughter	practical

Exercise 49.1
Draw lines to match the words to their pictures.

1. mus<u>ician</u>

2. electr<u>ician</u>

3. phys<u>ician</u>

4. beaut<u>ician</u>

5. mag<u>ician</u>

6. mathemat<u>ician</u>

7. poli<u>tician</u>

8. opt<u>ician</u>

Exercise 49.2
Complete the sentences with the words that make sense.

nutritious	musician	daughter	electrician
style	famous	imitation	poisonous

1. The _____ magician was at the show.

2. The _____ came to fix the light switch.

3. The fake diamond was a poor _____.

4. Watch out for the _____ snake!

5. The dietician will create a _____ meal.

6. I went to the beautician to get a new hair _____.

7. The _____ played the violin.

8. She taught her _____ how to swim.

Exercise 49.3
Circle the sound for the letters that are underlined.

1. phobia	/f/	/p/
2. chef	/k/	/sh/
3. mechanic	/k/	/sh/
4. picture	/tor/	/chur/
5. dangerous	/shus/	/us/

Exercise 49.4

Circle the sound for the letter(s) that are underlined.

1.	m<u>i</u>nd	long 'e'	long 'i'
2.	<u>eig</u>ht	long 'e'	long 'a'
3.	phob<u>i</u>a	long 'e'	long 'i'
4.	s<u>igh</u>	long 'i'	short 'e'
5.	h<u>ea</u>lth	long 'e'	short 'e'
6.	r<u>ea</u>dy	long 'e'	short 'e'
7.	gr<u>ea</u>t	long 'e'	long 'a'
8.	hell<u>o</u>	short 'o'	long 'o'

Exercise 49.5

Write the past tense form of the words below. Use the sentence: "Today I ___, but yesterday I ___."

aught / ought

1. teach _____

2. fight _____

3. catch _____

4. think _____

5. buy _____

Assign the dictations for this lesson,
and have your student play the on-line games for review.

Words from the French

1) Review the flash cards.

2) Check the dictations from the previous lesson.

The English language, as we know it today, wasn't around until the year 1500AD (that's only about 500 years ago). Before that, the people of England spoke different dialects and were influenced by the people who invaded their land.

The French invaded England in 1066AD, bringing with them their language. For a while, the English were only allowed to speak French, which didn't last long. However, many French words stayed, and today, more than 30% of our words are of French origin. In this lesson we're going to see some words that are different and don't follow our rules.

'et' as long 'a'	ballet bouquet filet	gourmet crochet sorbet	valet cabaret duvet

The French do not pronounce the 'h' at the beginning of a word. We saw some of these words already.

silent 'h'	heir honest	honor hour

The French also do not pronounce 'ou' as /ou/ as in "ouch". Instead, 'ou' is /oo/, as in "spooky boo".

'ou' as /oo/	group soup	croup wound

Read the following sentences:

1. The ballet dancer received a bouquet of flowers.

2. The gourmet chef made a filet of fish dinner.

3. For dessert, we had orange sorbet.

4. The honest boy couldn't tell a lie.

5. Our dining group had mushroom soup.

Exercise 50.1
Write the un-contracted words on the lines below.

1. couldn't _____

2. didn't _____

3. that's _____

4. they've _____

5. weren't _____

6. you've _____

Exercise 50.2
Circle the words where 'et' has the long 'a' sound (there are 6).

fillet	basket	ratchet
quiet	crochet	gourmet
ballet	bouquet	valet

Exercise 50.3
Circle the words where 'ea' has the short 'e' sound (there are 5).

dr<u>ea</u>m   l<u>ea</u>ther   l<u>ea</u>f

p<u>ea</u>k   ch<u>ea</u>t   br<u>ea</u>d

d<u>ea</u>f   w<u>ea</u>ther   spr<u>ea</u>d

Exercise 50.4
Circle the correct word for each sentence. Be careful, these are homophones, and you may not know which one to use.

1. The strong boy lifted the <u>weight / wait</u> over his head.

2. The wind <u>blue / blew</u> the door open.

3. The <u>some / sum</u> of one plus one is two.

4. The girl dressed up as a <u>which / witch</u> for Halloween.

5. The young couple drove down the <u>rode / road</u>.

6. The group <u>new / knew</u> how to find the train station.

Exercise 50.5
Circle the words that have the /f/ sound for the underlined letters (there are 6).

bou<u>gh</u>t   enou<u>gh</u>   dau<u>gh</u>ter   cou<u>gh</u>   tou<u>gh</u>

rou<u>gh</u>   <u>ph</u>ony   lau<u>gh</u>   cau<u>gh</u>t   brou<u>gh</u>t

Exercise 50.6
Circle the correct word(s) for each sentence.

 You may have to help your student determine the correct homophone. Knowing these will come with more practice as well as reading.

1. The little boy drew on the <u>piece / peace</u> of paper.

2. The <u>pore / poor</u> man begged for some money.

3. Don't <u>waste / waist</u> the expensive steak.

4. The money was <u>due / do / dew</u> at the meeting.

5. The boy <u>rights / writes</u> with his <u>right / write</u> hand.

6. The play-set is <u>made / maid</u> of <u>wood / would</u>.

7. I <u>herd / heard</u> that you ate the <u>whole / hole</u> pie!

8. The <u>sun / son</u> was <u>hi / high</u> in the sky.

Exercise 50.7
Circle the words where the 'h' is silent (there are 3).

<u>h</u>ip   <u>h</u>onor   <u>h</u>ockey

<u>h</u>ello   <u>h</u>amburger   <u>h</u>istory

<u>h</u>our   <u>h</u>orrible   <u>h</u>onest

 Assign the dictations for this lesson, and have your student play the on-line games for review.

Review
Lessons 41-50

1) Review the flash cards.
2) Check the dictations from the previous lesson.

 ## Read the words below.

halo	phobia	serious	laugh	magician
solo	pressure	arrive	cough	fillet
radio	vulture	Chicago	caught	hour
studio	famous	technical	fought	group

Exercise R5.1
Add apostrophes for ownership to the missing words.

1. _____ joke made me laugh!
   Jane

2. _____ turtle was caught trying to escape.
   Amy

3. The _____ cage needed to be cleaned.
   gerbils (more than one)

4. A rabbit was hiding in the _____ hat.
   magician

5. The_____ room needed to be cleaned.
   sisters (more than one)

Exercise R5.2
Circle the sound that the underlined letter(s) make.

1.	bacter<u>ia</u>	long 'i'	'e' - /uh/
2.	rad<u>io</u>	long 'i'	'e' - 'o'
3.	tax<u>i</u>	long 'e'	long 'i'
4.	stud<u>io</u>	long 'i'	'e' - 'o'
5.	Americ<u>a</u>	/uh/	long 'a'
6.	Chicag<u>o</u>	/oo/	long 'o'
7.	Alask<u>a</u>	/uh/	long 'a'

Exercise R5.3
Circle the words that complete the sentences.

1. The magician through / threw knives at his assistant.

2. The vulture flew / flu out of it's / its nest.

3. The angry boy went an hour / our without talking.

4. The ballet dancer wore a tutu around her waist / waste.

5. The chef made / maid a fish fillet dinner.

6. The famous actor passed / past by us without stopping.

7. The technician new / knew how to fix the radio.

Exercise R5.4
Unscramble the letters to complete the words.

1.

g   u
a   h

l__ __ __ __

5.

h   p
   o
e   n

micro__ __ __ __ __

2.

abcdefg
hijklmnop
qrstuv
wxyz

h   p
   a

al__ __ __ bet

6.

a   r   p
g   h

bar__ __ __ __ __

3.

u   o
g   h

c__ __ __ __ syrup

7.

i   p
h   n

dol__ __ __ __

4.

h   y
p   o

tr__ __ __ __

8.

h   p
   a
t   n

ele__ __ __ __ __

Exercise R5.5
Complete the sentences with the words that make sense.

culture   pasture   temperature   curious   mixture

1. The _____ cat opened the lid to investigate.

2. The drink is a _____ of soda and fruit juice.

3. The cows grazed out in the _____.

4. If you visit another country, you'll see their _____.

5. A thermometer tells you the current _____.

Exercise R5.6
Read each word out loud, and circle the sound that the underlined letters make.

1.	plea<u>se</u>	/z/	/s/
2.	relea<u>se</u>	/z/	/s/
3.	nerv<u>ous</u>	/us/	/s/
4.	lo<u>se</u>	/z/	/s/
5.	loo<u>se</u>	/z/	/s/
6.	me<u>ch</u>anic	/k/	/sh/
7.	ball<u>et</u>	long 'i'	long 'a'

Answers

Exercise 1.1: 1) saw, 2, duck, 3) pumpkin, 4) whistle, 5) ghost, 6) house, 7) jar, 8) zebra, 9) top, 10) rabbit, 11) yoyo, 12) kite, 13) vacuum, 14) nest, 15) fan, 16) ball, 17) cat, 18) mushroom, 19) lamp
Exercise 1.2: The vowels should be circled, a e i o u
Exercise 1.3: 1) elephant – e, 2) igloo – I, 3) apple – a, 4) umbrella – u, 5) octopus – o
Exercise 1.4: 1) axe – a, 2) elbow – e, 3) ostrich – o, 4) umpire – u
Exercise 1.5: 1) i, 2) e, 3) u, 4) a, 5) o

Exercise 2.1: 1) pin, 2) tub, 3) bat, 4) fox
Exercise 2.2: 1) bat, 2) net, 3) frog, 4) sock
Exercise 2.3: 1) net, 2) rug, 3) hen, 4) man
Exercise 2.4: 1) My, 2) have, 3) was, 4) do, 5) said
Exercise 2.5: 1) you, 2) does, 3) She, 4) Who, 5) go, 6) Where, 7) your

Exercise 3.1: 1) cup, 2) fan, 3) pot, 4) cap or hat, 5) bun, 6) lip
Exercise 3.2: 1) ten, 2) van, 3) box, 4) mop, 5) sun, 6) pig
Exercise 3.3: 1) was, 2) has, 3) They, 4) What, 5) does
Exercise 3.4: 1) bat, 2) vest, 3) milk, 4) bug, 5) mitt, 6) mop
Exercise 3.5: 1) pen, 2) bat, 3) bug, 4) lid, 5) bun, 6) mop, 7) pan, 8) tub, 9) pin, 10) dog
Exercise 3.6: 1) my, 2) They, 3) has, 4) does, 5) was
Exercise 3.7: tent, 2) fist, 3) frog, 4) belt
Exercise 3.8: 1) man, 2) rug, 3) net, 4) hug, 5) hen, 6) fox, 7) can, 8) hat
Exercise 3.9: (self explanatory)

Exercise 4.1: 1) pen, 2) cup, 3) box, 4) fan
Exercise 4.2: 1) stamp, 2) plant, 3) twins, 4) swim, 5) flat, 6) truck, 7) drip, 8) tree, 9) broom, 10) clock
Exercise 4.3: 1) stump, 2) tent, 3) list, 4) lamp, 5) plant, 6) hump, 7) milk, 8) belt
Exercise 4.4: 1) twig, 2) swim, 3) plug, 4) trip, 5) grin
Exercise 4.5: 1) desk, 2) help, 3) cup, 4) ask, 5) fast, 6) held

Exercise 5.1: 1) hatch, 2) crutch, 3) switch, 4) latch, 5) scratch
Exercise 5.2: 1) chin, 2) chip, 3) chimp, 4) rich, 5) stitch, 6) pitch
Exercise 5.3: 1) sketch, 2) batch, 3) clutch, 4) notch, 5) snatch, 6) fetch
Exercise 5.4: 1) lash, 2) crash, 3) brush, 4) stash, 5) hush
Exercise 5.5: 1) crash, 2) shut, 3) chat, 4) cash, 5) rash, 6) punch, 7) champ, 8) bash, 9) such

Exercise 6.1: 1) wish, 2) snitch, 3) rash, 4) path, 5) snatch, 6) flush
Exercise 6.2: 1) path, 2) flash, 3) slash, 4) chin, 5) thin
Exercise 6.3: 1) lash, 2) patch, 3) math, 4) switch, 5) path, 6) fish, 7) bath, 8) brush, 9) match, 10) crash
Exercise 6.4: 1) He, 2) of, 3) The, 4) My, 5) Was, 6) you
Exercise 6.5: 1) nest, 2) thin, 3) lost, 4) math, 5) wish, 6) bath
Exercise 6.6: 1) blast, 2) slap, 3) fast, 4) trip, 5) that

Exercise 7.1: 1) drip, 2) drank, 3) drop, 4) drag, 5) drink
Exercise 7.2: 1) short, 2) long, 3) short, 4) long, 5) long, 6) long
Exercise 7.3: 1) has, 2) does, 3) have, 4) of, 5) do
Exercise 7.4: 1) pink, 2) plank, 3) crank, 4) yank, 5) link, 6) rash, 7) chunk, 8) splash, 9) crash, 10) junk
Exercise 7.5: 1) tank, 2) pink, 3) drink, 4) sink, 5) trunk, 6) bank

Exercise 8.1: was, his, is, has
Exercise 8.2: 1) thank, 2) honk, 3) bunk, 4) chunk, 5) rink
Exercise 8.3: 1) crank, 2) blink, 3) strong, 4) string, 5) chunk, 6) clung
Exercise 8.4: 1) sing, 2) long, 3) song, 4) ring, 5) stung, 6) hang
Exercise 8.5: 1) wink, 2) king, 3) lung, 4) tank, 5) strong, 6) sing, 7) trunk, 8) drink, 9) ring, 10) sink, 11) wing, 12) skunk

Answers

Exercise 9.1: 1) trick, 2) luck, 3) back, 4) stuck, 5) brick, 6) stack
Exercise 9.2: 1) trust, 2) drink, 3) drip, 4) drag, 5) trip, 6) drop, 7) trap, 8) drank
Exercise 9.3: 1) sock, 2) snack, 3) sick, 4) rock, 5) duck, 6) truck, 7) clock, 8) block, 9) tack, 10) kick
Exercise 9.4: 1) pack, 2) switch, 3) snack, 4) snuck, 5) truck, 6) drink, 7) trick, 8) stick
Exercise 9.5: 1) is, 2) the, 3) to, 4) have

Exercise 10.1: 1) back, 2) stay, 3) check, 4) pack, 5) way, 6) may
Exercise 10.2: 1) pray, 2) tack, 3) tray, 4) ring, 5) crutch, 6) sock, 7) lung, 8) wing, 9) duck, 10) truck
Exercise 10.3: 1) prank, 2) play, 3) shrank, 4) strong, 5) stick
Exercise 10.4: 1) stray, 2) sway, 3) play, 4) clay, 5) stay, 6) day, 7) pay
Exercise 10.5: 1a) black, 3a) rich, 4a) spring, 1d) back, 2d) drink

Review 1.1: 1) box, 2) ship, 3) ring, 4) fan, 5) fish
Review 1.2: 1) brick, 2) clock, 3) tack, 4) truck, 5) catch, 6) brush
Review 1.3: (match to the pictures)
Review 1.4: 1) lung, 2) trash, 3) think, 4) back, 5) stop
Review 1.5: 1d) catch, 3d) strong, 4d) stamp, 2a) tent, 4a) scratch, 5a) bank

Exercise 11.1: 1) bloom – gloom, 2) group – hoop, 3) flood – blood, 4) took – shook, 5) stood – good
Exercise 11.2: 1) black, 2) foot, 3) play, 4) frog, 5) food, 6) hook
Exercise 11.3: 1) good, 2) hook, 3) shook, 4) took, 5) look
Exercise 11.4: 1) moon, 2) noon, 3) bedroom, 4) broom, 5) bloom, 6) soon
Exercise 11.5: 1) moon, 2) spoon, 3) broom, 4) foot, 5) hook, 6) book
Exercise 11.6: 1) broom, 2) shelf, 3) shook, 4) long, 5) spoon, 6) sun

Exercise 12.1: 1) quick, 2) stay, 3) shrank, 4) think, 5) quest
Exercise 12.2: 1) away, 2) play, 3) trick, 4) good, 5) broom, 6) quick
Exercise 12.3: 1) quick, 2) quack, 3) spoon, 4) broom, 5) food, 6) quit
Exercise 12.4: (see pictures)

Exercise 13.1: 1) wrench, 2) pinch, 3) bench, 4) branch, 5) lunch, 6) inch
Exercise 13.2: 1) zoo, 2) pinch, 3) branch, 4) sick, 5) crack, 6) stuck, 7) blank
Exercise 13.3: 1) hatch, 2) back, 3) luck, 4) fetch, 5) shrank, 6) strong
Exercise 13.4: 1) punch, 2) pinch, 3) branch, 4) stitch, 5) black, 6) sway
Exercise 13.5: 1) trick, 2) bench, 3) book, 4) pinch, 5) good

Exercise 14.1: 1) try, 2) night, 3) cry, 4) shy, 5) right, 6) by, 7) Why, 8) fly
Exercise 14.2: 1) think, 2) thigh, 3) thing, 4) shy, 5) shack, 6) shock
Exercise 14.3: 1) high, 2) night, 3) dry, 4) bright, 5) right
Exercise 14.4: 1) tank, 2) stuck, 3) bunk, 4) sock, 5) stick
Exercise 14.5: draw lines to pictures

Exercise 15.1: 1) boil, 2) bench, 3) tinfoil, 4) boys, 5) soil, 6) drank, 7) tool, 8) toys
Exercise 15.2: 1) coin, 2) switch, 3) toybox, 4) boy, 5) patch, 6) point, 7) drink, 8) coil
Exercise 15.3: 1) fish, 2) bucket, 3) broil, 4) bed, 5) coin, 6) hoops, 7) pool
Exercise 15.4: 1) tight, 2) boil, 3) joy, 4) tool, 5) tooth

Exercise 16.1: 1) star, 2) car, 3) barn, 4) jar, 5) shark, 6) chart, 7) cards, 8) arm
Exercise 16.2: 1) corn, 2) store, 3) core, 4) thorn, 5) snore, 6) horse, 7) horn, 8) score
Exercise 16.3: draw lines to match
Exercise 16.4: 1) store, 2) marker, 3) more, 4) church, 5) turn, 6) shore, 7) curb
Exercise 16.5: door, floor, poor, your, four
Exercise 16.6: 1) were, 2) was, 3) We're, 4) was, 5) were

Exercise 17.1: draw lines to match
Exercise 17.2: circle the corresponding picture
Exercise 17.3: 1) town, 2) storm, 3) smart, 4) about, 5) curb, 6) tray, 7) tooth
Exercise 17.4: 1) pool, 2) cloud, 3) stout, 4) row, 5) blow, 6) far
Exercise 17.5: 1) ground, 2) stool, 3) were, 4) crowd, 5) lost, 6) own, 7) snow, 8) lunch, 9) house, 10) shower

Exercise 18.1: 1) born, 2) town, 3) grew, 4) flew, 5) screw
Exercise 18.2: 1) could, 2) threw, 3) flew, 4) shower, 5) crew, 6) bowl, 7) drew
Exercise 18.3: 1) turn, 2) crowd, 3) blew, 4) boil, 5) howl, 6) grew
Exercise 18.4: try, right, high
Exercise 18.5: 1) er/ir, 2) ew/oo, 3) ou/ow, 4) ur/ir, 5) oi/oy
Exercise 18.6: could, stood, should, hood

Exercise 19.1: 1) take, 2) stake, 3) lake, 4) rack, 5) bake, 6) snack
Exercise 19.2: 1.) pota, 2) stimog, 3) amibr, 4) opit, 5) umotx, 6) imat, 7) lobut, 8) flita
Exercise 19.3: 1) fine, 2) tub, 3) rode, 4) kite, 5) rip, 6) shine, 7) kit, 8) tube, 9) shin, 10) fin
Exercise 19.4: ai, ee & ea, ie, oa, ue
Exercise 19.5: 1) boat, 2) nail, 3) pie, 4) true, 5) rain, 6) tail, 7) float, 8) pain, 9) stain, 10) blue
Exercise 19.6: 1) quiet, 2) suit, 3) lion, 4) ruin, 5) poem, 6) fruit
Exercise 19.7: 1) queen, 2) yard, 3) bird, 4) joint, 5) snout, 6) fingernails
Exercise 19.8: 1) flew & flow, 2) grew & grown, 3) chore & chew

Exercise 20.1: ai, ee & ea, ie, oa, ue
Exercise 20.2: 1) hitting, 2) biting, 3) hoping, 4) hopping, 5) sipping
Exercise 20.3: 1) tree, 2) pie, 3) snake, 4) tape, 5) tail, 6) train, 7) pail, 8) tie
Exercise 20.4: 1) taking, 2) parting, 3) crying, 4) sitting, 5) petting, 6) liking, 7) melting, 8) singing
Exercise 20.5: 1) ay & ai, 2) ee & ea, 3) igh & ie, 4) oa, 5) ue

Review 2.1: 1) inch, 2) stew, 3) slide, 4) ground, 5) road
Review 2.2: 1) shirt, 2) store, 3) third, 4) were, 5) turn, 6) first
Review 2.3: 1) pipe, 2) tape, 3) cone, 4) rake, 5) snake, 6) robe, 7) teeth, 8) rain, 9) boat, 10) snail, 11) glue, 12) three
Review 2.4: 1) feel, 2) real, 3) week, 4) sleep, 5) street
Review 2.5: 1) barn, 2) corn, 3) star, 4) jar, 5) bow, 6) spoon, 7) broom, 8) crown
Review 2.6: 1) sleeping, 2) clapping, 3) drinking, 4) running, 5) sitting, 6) catching

Exercise 21.1: 1) /t/, 2) /ed/, 3) /t/, 4) /t/, 5) /t/, 6) /t/, 7) /t/, 8) /t/, 9) /ed/, 10) /ed/
Exercise 21.2: 1) skipped, 2) shopped, 3) planned, 4) ripped, 5) dragged
Exercise 21.3: 1) crying, 2) cried, 3) tried, 4) trying, 5) fried, 6) frying
Exercise 21.4: 1) eat – ate, 2) make – made, 3) shake – shook, 4) fly – flew, 5) draw – drew, 6) take – took, 7) keep – kept, 8) dig – dug
Exercise 21.5: 1) poked, 2) played, 3) waited, 4) watched, 5) baked, 6) trimmed

Exercise 22.1: 1) stand, 2) pond, 3) find, 4) under, 5) spend
Exercise 22.2: 1) We're, 2) we're, 3) were, 4) Were, 5) Where
Exercise 22.3: 1) oa, 2) ow, 3) ow, 4) ai, 5) ay, 6) igh
Exercise 22.4: 1) pinned, 2) running, 3) jumped, 4) landed, 5) winning
Exercise 22.5: fly, sight, child, wild, cry, find
Exercise 22.6: 1) rain, 2) shirt, 3) jumped, 4) hurt, 5) shopped, 6) return, 7) cloud, 8) town, 9) were, 10) street
Exercise 22.7: higip   guebt   bito

Answers

Exercise 23.1: 1) Conn_ect_, 2) _act_ing, 3) sel_ect_, 4) pred_ict_, 5) sus_pect_, 6) e_ject_ed
Exercise 23.2: 1) licked, 2) backed, 3) pact, 4) cracked
Exercise 23.3: 1) slipped, 2) tried, 3) found, 4) acted, 5) running, 6) took, 7) spied, 8) skipped, 9) packed, 10) flew
Exercise 23.4: Circle the corresponding pictures.

Exercise 24.1: Draw lines to match the pictures.
Exercise 24.2: Draw lines to match the pictures.
Exercise 24.3: 1) fault, 2) walk, 3) ball, 4) awful, 5) pause
Exercise 24.4: 1) igh – ie, 2) aw – au, 3) oy – oi, 4) ew – oo, 5) ay – ai, 6) ur – er
Exercise 24.5: 1) author, 2) because, 3) subject, 4) dawn, 5) predict, 6) lawn, 7) launch

Exercise 25.1: Draw lines to match the pictures.
Exercise 25.2: 1) h_orse_, 2) h_ouse_, 3) n_urse_, 4) m_ouse_
Exercise 25.3: 1) mouse, 2) please, 3) horse, 4) house, 5) noise, 6) chose, 7) close
Exercise 25.4: 1) using, 2) cried, 3) used, 4) stopped, 5) closing
Exercise 25.5: these, those, use, his, because, wise, pause
Exercise 25.6: 1) clawed, 2) coiled, 3) choosing, 4) acting, 5) crawled
Exercise 25.7: 1) aw – au, 2) oi – oy, 3) oo – ew, 4) ou – ow, 5) ie – igh

Exercise 26.1: 1) type, 2) cozy, 3) bakery, 4) supply, 5) noisy, 6) sneaky, 7) mystery
Exercise 26.2: Draw lines to match the pictures. At the end of a word, 'y' can sound like a long 'e', or long 'i'.
Exercise 26.3: 1) scary, 2) deny, 3) rely, 4) dry, 5) satisfy, 6) pry, 7) plenty, 8) hurry, 9) modify, 10) crazy / long 'i' or short 'i'.

Exercise 27.1: 1) normally, 2) finally, 3) safely, 4) luckily, 5) angrily, 6) happily
Exercise 27.2: 1) library, 2) bottle, 3) soup, 4) song, 5) sandwiches
Exercise 27.3: 1) hotter, 2) bigger, 3) fatter, 4) hitter, 5) jogger
Exercise 27.4: 1) happier, 2) funnier, 3) uglier, 4) sorrier, 5) prettier

Exercise 28.1: 1) /j/, 2) /g/, 3) /g/, 4) /j/
Exercise 28.2: 1) ju_dge_, 2) bri_dge_, 3) le_dge_, 4) slu_dge_, 5) ple_dge_, 6) ba_dge_, 7) we_dge_, 8) gru_dge_
Exercise 28.3: 1) stage, 2) huge, 3) edge, 4) wedge, 5) judge
Exercise 28.4: 1) changing, 2) arrange, 3) revenge, 4) strangers, 5) angle, 6) cringed
Exercise 28.5: 1) cri_nge_, 2) arra_nge_, 3) stra_nge_, 4) twi_nge_, 5) plu_nge_, 6) lu_nge_, 7) bi_nge_, 8) fri_nge_
Exercise 28.6: 1) fu_dge_, 2) plu_nge_r, 3) a_nge_l, 4) fri_dge_, 5) bri_dge_, 6) ba_dge_

Exercise 29.1: 1) percent, 2) advice, 3) chance, 4) place, 5) price
Exercise 29.2: 1) place, 2) face, 3) race & rice, 4) space & spice, 5) grace, 6) slice, 7) advice, 8) pace
Exercise 29.3: 1) glance, 2) chance & change, 3) prance, 4) range, 5) trance
Exercise 29.4: 1) race, 2) slice, 3) face, 4) since, 5) space, 6) dance, 7) nice, 8) fence, 9) advice, 10) Place
Exercise 29.5: 1) dancing, 2) received, 3) pranced, 4) advancing, 5) traced
Exercise 29.6: raged   forged   energy   gerbil

Exercise 30.1: 1) skill, 2) kind, 3) clap, 4) traffic, 5) picnic, 6) keep, 7) clear, 8) camp
Exercise 30.2: 1) ks, 2) s, 3) s, 4) ks, 5) ks, 6) ks
Exercise 30.3: 1) attic, 2) garlic, 3) panic, 4) fantastic, 5) plastic, 6) romantic, 7) traffic, 8) magic

Review 3.1: 1) ce - /s/, 2) au - /aw/, 3) adge - /aj/, 4) alk - /awk/, 5) all - /awl/
Review 3.2: 1d) claws, 2d) predict, 3a) pause, 4a) false, 5a) fault
Review 3.3: 1) doctor, 2) chalk, 3) law, 4) traffic, 5) talk, 6) symbol
Review 3.4: 1) e, i, y , 2) e, i, y, 3) long 'i' or short 'i', 4) long 'e' or long 'i'
Review 3.5: 1) ju_dge_, 2) c_age_, 3) ba_dge_, 4) bri_dge_, 5) bo_unce_, 6) pen_cil_, 7) jui_ce_, 8) pri_ce_
Review 3.6: 1) softly, 2) swiftly, 3) lately, 4) easily, 5) finally, 6) luckily
Review 3.7: 1) space, 2) chance, 3) force, 4) city, 5) fence, 6) choice, 7) principal, 8) race

Exercise 31.1: 1) boxes, 2) lashes, 3) wolves, 4) puppies, 5) houses, 6) cherries, 7) ladies, 8) tries
Exercise 31.2: 1) boxes, 2) days, 3) leaves, 4) wishes, 5) stories
Exercise 31.3: 1) mystery, 2) stranger, 3) advice, 4) berries
Exercise 31.4: 1) taxes, 2) bushes, 3) lashes, 4) memories, 5) stories
Exercise 31.5: 1) /k/, 2) /s/, 3) /s/, 4) /k/, 5) /j/, 6) /g/, 7) /j/, 8) /j/

Exercise 32.1: 1) 2, 2) 2, 3) 1, 4) 3, 5) 2, 6) 2, 7) 3, 8) 3
Exercise 32.2: 1) drill, 2) dress, 3) spill, 4) hill, 5) boss, 6) well, 7) pill, 8) bell
Exercise 32.3: 1) useless, 2) mattress, 3) witness, 4) recess, 5) careless, 6) spotless
Exercise 32.4: 1) told, 2) held, 3) posted, 4) folded, 5) sold, 6) rolled
Exercise 32.5: 1) berries, 2) scarves, 3) children, 4) well, 5) bold, 6) flurries
Exercise 32.6: 1) old, 2) hold, 3) gold, 4) folder, 5) roll / fls

Exercise 33.1: 1) message, 2) advantage, 3) package, 4) baggage, 5) practice, 6) notice, 7) stage, 8) average
Exercise 33.2: 1) i, 2) i, 3) o, 4) o, 5) i, 6) o, 7) i, 8) i, 9) i, 10) o
Exercise 33.3: 1) stories, 2) ladies, 3) cities, 4) deliveries, 5) families, 6) factories
Exercise 33.4: 1) alligators, 2) refrigerator, 3) amusement, 4) mythical, 5) compound, 6) convincing
Exercise 33.5: 1) planned, 2) took, 3) sold, 4) ran, 5) woke, 6) ate, 7) went, 8) hoped

Exercise 34.1: 1) I'm – I am, 2) I'll – I will, 3) I've – I have, 4) haven't – have not, 5) they're – they are, 6) they've – they have, 7) he's – he is, 8) didn't – did not, 9) doesn't – does not, 10) she's – she is
Exercise 34.2: 1) They're, 2) doesn't, 3) she's, 4) I'm, 5) weren't
Exercise 34.3: 1) wouldn't, 2) they're, 3) We've, 4) haven't, 5) shouldn't, 6) We're
Exercise 34.4: 1) sniff, 2) bell, 3) drill, 4) miss, 5) skill, 6) less, 7) spilled, 8) stuff, 9) pill, 10) full

Exercise 35.1: 1) won/one, 2) whole/hole, 3) hear/here, 4) sent/scent, 5) maid/made, 6) two/too
Exercise 35.2: 1) They're, 2) their, 3) their, 4) there, 5) There, 6) there, 7) they're, 8) Their, 9) there, 10) their
Exercise 35.3: 1) to, 2) too, 3) too, to, 4) two, 5) to
Exercise 35.4: 1) fourth, 2) scent, 3) sent, mail, 4) male, 5) won
Exercise 35.5: 1) meet, 2) buy, 3) poor, 4) see, 5) hear, 6) cent, 7) fourth, 8) threw
Exercise 35.6: 1) can't, 2) don't, 3) it's, 4) she'll, 5) she's
Exercise 35.7: 1) runner, 2) easier, 3) colder, 4) wetter, 5) happier, 6) nicer, 7) fatter, 8) thinner

Exercise 36:1: 1) whined, 2) wheel, 3) whimper, 4) whisper, 5) whale
Exercise 36.2: 1) knee, 2) knit, 3) thumb, 4) lamb, 5) comb, 6) knife, 7) bomb, 8) island
Exercise 36.3: 1) night, 2) write, 3) sight, 4) no, 5) high, 6) hour, 7) new, 8) whole
Exercise 36.4: 1) knight, 2) two, 3) sword, 4) autumn, 5) wrong, 6) write
Exercise 36.5: 1) ghost, 2) whale, 3) knight, 4) autumn, 5) sword, 6) two, 7) whistle, 8) wrong, 9) write
Exercise 36.6: 1) numb, 2) write, 3) whistle, 4) knob, 5) autumn

Exercise 37.1: 1) chief, 2) cookie, 3) genie, 4) movie, 5) hoodie, 6) doggie, 7) eight, 8) brownie, 9) bootie, 10) birdie
Exercise 37.2: 1) believe, 2) relief, 3) field, 4) pieces, 5) freight, 6) genie
Exercise 37.3: 1) weight, 2) brief, 3) eight, 4) achieve, 5) neighbor
Exercise 37.4: 1) free, 2) seen, 3) field, 4) eight, 5) fight, 6) neighbor, 7) brief, 8) cookie, 9) relief, 10) keep, 11) belief, 12) receive
Exercise 37.5: 1) i, 2) a, 3) i, 4) a, 5) e, 6) i, 7) a, 8) e

Answers

Exercise 38.1: 1) measure, 2) treasure, 3) feathers, 4) heavy, 5) heaven, 6) sweater
Exercise 38.2: Draw lines to pictures
Exercise 38.3: 1) pear, 2) steak, 3) bear, 4) tear
Exercise 38.4: 1) said, 2) against, 3) mountain, 4) certain, 5) again
Exercise 38.5: 1) head – bed, 2) eight – state, 3) limb – him, 4) sign – fine, 5) comb – foam, 6) right – spite, 7) field – sealed, 8) grief – leaf
Exercise 38.6: 1) said/bread, 2) great/plate, 3) eight/late, 4) sweater/wetter, 5) leather/weather

Exercise 39.1: 1) official, 2) special, 3) confidential, 4) initially, 5) facial, 6) residential
Exercise 39.2: field   cookie   movie
Exercise 39.3: 1) long 'e', 2) long 'e', 3) short 'e', 4) long 'e', 5) long 'i', 6) short 'e', 7) long 'a', 8) short 'e'
Exercise 39.4: 1) climb – chime, 2) numb – gum, 3) known – groan, 4) which – pitch, 5) tight – bite, 6) head – led, 7) doubt – spout
Exercise 39.5: 1a) one, 4a) hour, 5a) thread, 2d) eight, 3d) alone

Exercise 40.1: Match words to their equations
Exercise 40.2: 1) mission, 2) lotion, 3) transportation, 4) solution, 5) caution
Exercise 40.3: 1) long 'a', 2) long 'i', 3) long 'a', 4) long 'a', 5) long 'e', 6) long 'e'
Exercise 40.4: 1) dictionary, 2) population, 3) professional, 4) definition, 5) relationship
Exercise 40.5: 1) condition, 2) missing, 3) audition, 4) truth, 5) field, 6) bread
Exercise 40.6: 1) pair, 2) pears, 3) steak, 4) stake, 5) grate, 6) great
Exercise 40.7: 1) long 'i', 2) short 'e', 3) short 'e', 4) long 'e', 5) long 'a'

Review 4.1: 1) answer, 2) doubt, 3) thumb, 4) toward, 5) wrong, 6) climb, 7) island, 8) crumb
Review 4.2: 1) batches, 2) wishes, 3) boxes, 4) cities, 5) knives
Review 4.3: 1) knee, 2) answer, 3) know, 4) knife, 5) knot, 6) knob
Review 4.4: 1) eight, 2) cookie, 3) bread, 4) pear, 5) sweater, 6) head, 7) bear, 8) wealthy
Review 4.5: 1) vision, 2) measure, 3) healthy, 4) wealthy, 5) nutrition
Review 4.6: 1) I will – I'll, 2) I am – I'm, 3) they are – they're, 4) they will – they'll, 5) it is – it's, 6) it will – it'll, 7) we have – we've, 8) we are – we're
Review 4.7: head   feather   heavy   ready   health

Exercise 41.1: 1) grandfather's, 2) baby's, 3) Jim's, 4) bird's, 5) father's, 6) Sam's, 7) Emily's, 8) dogs'
Exercise 41.2: 1) dog's, 2) none, 3) John's, 4) students', 5) Jill's
Exercise 41.3: 1) it's, 2) they're, 3) we're, 4) their, 5) there, 6) Were
Exercise 41.4: 1) tion-sion, 2)oy-oi, 3) ew-oo, 4) cial-tial, 5) oa-ow, 6) ee-ea, 7) ai-ay, 8) ie-igh, 9) er-ur, 10) aw-au
Exercise 41.5: 1) motion, 2) question, 3) celebration, 4) definition, 5) operation
Exercise 41.6: 1) Jade's, 2) Amy's, 3) Joey's, 4) Mary's, 5) teacher's, 6) boys'
Exercise 41.7: weight   raining   braid   tank

Exercise 42.1: 1) long 'o', 2) /uh/, 3) 'e'-'o', 4) 'e'-'o', 5) /uh/, 6) long 'o', 7) long 'o', 8) /uh/
Exercise 42.2: 1) tornado, 2) bacteria, 3) tomato, 4) family, 5) America
Exercise 42.3: 1) tuna, 2) taxi, 3) zero, 4) radio, 5) sofa, 6) comma, 7) extra
Exercise 42.4: 1) zebra, 2) pizza, 3) taxi, 4) radio, 5) tuba, 6) panda, 7) potato, 8) tomato
Exercise 42.5: 1) helium, 2) broccoli, 3) period, 4) medium, 5) experience, 6) medium, 7) ingredient, 8) pita, 9) stadium, 10) historian

Exercise 43.1: 1) candle, 2) handle, 3) ankle, 4) turtle
Exercise 43.2: 1) kettle, 2) apple, 3) puzzle, 4) bubble, 5) bottle, 6) waffle
Exercise 43.3: 1) puddle, 2) apple, 3) bottle, 4) handle, 5) cuddle, 6) curable, 7) flexible
Exercise 43.4: 1) noodles, 2) stable, 3) visible, 4) ankle, 5) possible
Exercise 43.5: 1) long 'e', 2) long 'a', 3) long 'i', 4) long 'a', 5) short 'e', 6) short 'e', 7) short 'e', 8) short 'e'

Exercise 44.1: 1) hallway, 2) paper, 3) future, 4) birds, 5) gym, 6) posture, 7) adventure
Exercise 44.2: 1) /chur/, 2) /shun/, 3) /shur/, 4) long 'i', 5) long 'a', 6) /shull/, 7) /shull/, 8) /shun/
Exercise 44.3: 1) mixture, 2) pasture, 3) temperature, 4) fractured, 5) punctured, 6) future
Exercise 44.4: 1) always, 2) sometimes, 3) long 'e', 4) 'i' sound, 5) no
Exercise 44.5: 1) stories, 2) ladies, 3) parties, 4) babies, 5) abilities, 6) bodies, 7) memories, 8) dictionaries

Exercise 45.1: 1) famous, 2) serious, 3) gorgeous, 4) curious, 5) dangerous
Exercise 45.2: 1) precious, 2) nutritious, 3) suspicious, 4) cautious, 5) anxious, 6) vicious, 7) gracious, 8) obnoxious
Exercise 45.3: 1) /us/, 2) 'e'-/us/, 3) /us/, 4) /shus/, 5) /shus/, 6) /us/, 7) 'e'-/us/, 8) /shus/
Exercise 45.4: 1) furious, 2) studio, 3) numerous, 4) Too, 5) obvious
Exercise 45.5: 1) ous-us, 2) oi-oy, 3) tial-shull, 4) tion-shun, 5) cial-shull, 6) eigh-'a', 7) igh-'i'
Exercise 45.6: 1) running, 2) slipping, 3) carrying, 4) identifying, 5) shaking, 6) breaking
Exercise 45.7: 1) mature, 2) equal, 3) delicious, 4) compassion, 5) mansion, 6) version, 7) obvious, 8) numerous, 9) dangerous, 10) cautious

Exercise 46.1: 1) expensive, 2) negative, 3) arrive, 4) talkative, 5) creative, 6) active, 7) festive
Exercise 46.2: 1) long 'i', 2) long 'i', 3) short 'i', 4) short 'i', 5) long 'i', 6) long 'i'
Exercise 46.3: 1) ve, 2) ge, 3) e, i, y, 4) e, i, y
Exercise 46.4: 1) knife – knives, 2) baby – babies, 3) watch – watches, 4) loaf – loaves
Exercise 46.5: 1) furniture, 2) lotion, 3) dangerous, 4) addition, 5) special

Exercise 47.1: Draw lines to match words to pictures.
Exercise 47.2: echo   mechanic   school   ache   chaos
Exercise 47.3: 1) stomach, 2) ache, 3) character, 4) chemicals, 5) chandelier
Exercise 47.4: 1) /k/, 2) /k/, 3) /sh/, 4) /ch/ as in "chop", 5) /k/, 6) /sh/, 7) /ch/ as in "chop", 8) /sh/, 9) /k/, 10) /k/
Exercise 47.5: 1) Fic<u>tion</u>, 2) fam<u>ous</u>, 3) edu<u>cation</u>, 4) stom<u>ach</u>, 5) scr<u>atch</u>, 6) br<u>igh</u>t, 7) pic<u>ture</u>, 8) act<u>ive</u>

Exercise 48.1: 1) phone, 2) sphere, 3) dolphin, 4) trophy, 5) microphone, 6) alphabet
Exercise 48.2: 1) enough, 2) graph, 3) rough, 4) tough, 5) cough, 6) laugh
Exercise 48.3: 1) <u>f</u>ought, 2) <u>th</u>ought, 3) <u>b</u>ought, 4) <u>br</u>ought
Exercise 48.4: 1) school, 2) subtract, 3) thought, 4) bought, 5) brought
Exercise 48.5: 1) ph - /f/, 2) igh – long 'i', 3) aught - /awt/, 4) sure - /shur/, 5) oi – oy, 6) ous - /us/, 7) ture - /chur/, 8) ve - /v/, 9) ge - /j/, 10) ce - /s/

Exercise 49.1: Draw lines to match words to pictures.
Exercise 49.2: 1) famous, 2) electrician, 3) imitation, 4) poisonous, 5) nutritious, 6) style, 7) musician, 8) daughter
Exercise 49.3: 1) /f/, 2) /sh/, 3) /k/, 4) /chur/, 5) /us/
Exercise 49.4: 1) long 'i', 2) long 'a', 3) long 'e', 4) long 'i', 5) short 'e', 6) short 'e', 7) long 'a', 8) long 'o'
Exercise 49.5: 1) taught, 2) fought, 3) caught, 4) thought, 5) bought

Exercise 50.1: 1) could not, 2) did not, 3) that is, 4) they have, 5) were not, 6) you have
Exercise 50.2: fillet   ballet   crochet   bouquet   gourmet   valet
Exercise 50.3: deaf   leather   weather   bread   spread
Exercise 50.4: 1) weight, 2) blew, 3) sum, 4) witch, 5) road, 6) knew
Exercise 50.5: rough   enough   phony   laugh   cough   tough
Exercise 50.6: 1) piece, 2) poor, 3) waste, 4) due, 5) writes, right, 6) made, wood, 7) heard, whole, 8) sun, high
Exercise 50.7: hour   honor   honest

Review 5.1: 1) Jane's, 2) Amy's, 3) gerbils', 4) magician's, 5) sisters'
Review 5.2: 1) 'e'-/uh/, 2) 'e'-'o', 3) long 'e', 4) 'e'-'o', 5) /uh/, 6) long 'o', 7) /uh/
Review 5.3: 1) threw, 2) flew, its, 3) hour, 4) waist, 5) made, 6) passed, 7) knew
Review 5.4: 1) <u>laugh</u>, 2) alphabet, 3) <u>cough</u> syrup, 4) tro<u>phy</u>, 5) micro<u>phone</u>, 6) bar-<u>graph</u>, 7) dol<u>phin</u>, 8) ele<u>phant</u>
Review 5.5: 1) curious, 2) mixture, 3) pasture, 4) culture, 5) temperature
Review 5.6: 1) /z/, 2) /s/, 3) /us/, 4) /z/, 5) /s/, 6) /k/, 7) long 'a'

- 267 -

Lesson 3

1. pot
2. pat
3. bit
4. hut
5. tip
6. pin
7. hub
8. lap
9. rub
10. rat

11. The cat is on my lap.
12. The rat is in the tub.
13. The dog is on the rug.

Important: make sure your student says the sounds as (s)he writes.

Lesson 4

1. slap
2. slip
3. milk
4. nest
5. brag
6. scab
7. help
8. twin
9. trot
10. drop

11. The frog will jump.
12. I went on a trip.
13. The fox was in the trap.

Lesson 5

1. chop
2. chip
3. champ
4. ship
5. hush
6. hatch
7. snitch
8. patch
9. batch
10. fish

11. Did you catch the frog?
12. He had a lot of cash.
13. I wish I had a pet chimp.
14. He has a rash on his leg.

Lesson 6

1. this
2. that
3. than
4. trash
5. with
6. patch
7. match
8. path
9. swish
10. thin

11. He went to the dump with the trash.
12. I had a bath in the tub.
13. You must do the math.
14. Put the cash in the box.

Lesson 7

1. sank
2. sink
3. stunk
4. prank
5. shrunk
6. bank
7. dunk
8. think
9. thank
10. blink

11. The pig is not fat, it is plump.
12. He had a lot of junk.
13. The skunk ran to me.
14. He drank the cup of broth.

Lesson 8

1. sang
2. sting
3. stung
4. song
5. long
6. lung
7. hang
8. hung
9. thing
10. string

11. The pig flung the mud at the dog.
12. The man was strong.
13. Bring the drink with you.

Important: have your student read what (s)he wrote by sounding out the sounds, and then make the correction

Lesson 9

1. tick
2. trick
3. stack
4. stick
5. track
6. speck
7. black
8. brick
9. sock
10. lock

11. The truck had a flat.
12. The duck swam on the pond.
13. His leg got stuck in the mud.
14. He has a bit of luck.

Lesson 10

1. you
2. me
3. do
4. may
5. ray
6. stay
7. day
8. lay
9. sway
10. clay
11. slay
12. crayon

13. We think you must go that way.
14. He is away at camp.
15. Today, I will catch a fish in the bay.

Lesson 11

1. loop
2. hoop
3. soon
4. broom
5. spoon
6. good
7. book
8. took
9. look
10. shook

11. Do not play a bad trick on me.
12. I want to jump in the pool.
13. It was a cool day.
14. I got mad and went to my room.

Lesson 12

1. quick
2. quit
3. quilt
4. quest
5. what
6. go
7. do
8. does

9. The wing of the duck got stuck.
10. The cat took the ham from the dish.
11. Bring him back as soon as you can.
12. He does not want to quit his job.

Lesson 13

1. bench
2. inch
3. punch
4. hunch
5. lunch
6. ranch
7. munch
8. drench
9. crunch
10. pinch

11. Do not pinch my chin!
12. The branch had a crack in it.
13. I had lunch at noon.
14. He sat on the bench to rest.

Lesson 14

1. try
2. fly
3. fry
4. cry
5. dry
6. by
7. pry
8. sly
9. shy
10. right
11. high
12. thigh
13. sigh
14. sight
15. might

Important: make sure your student says the sounds as (s)he writes

Lesson 15

1. soil
2. coil
3. boil
4. tinfoil
5. boy
6. toy
7. ploy
8. soy
9. broil
10. joy

1. Why was the boy sad?
2. The boy will point to the sky.
3. The man will broil the fish.
4. I had one coin in my pocket.

Lesson 16

1. were
2. her
3. winter
4. under
5. sister
6. shorter
7. longer
8. start
9. born
10. cart

11. The star was in the sky.
12. Do not burn your finger on the hot pot.
13. The car went faster and then hit the curb.
14. Do not forget to stir the soup.

Lesson 17

1. show
2. shown
3. blow
4. blown
5. town
6. pound
7. shout
8. pout
9. flow
10. flower

11. The dog will not growl at you.
12. In the winter it may snow.
13. The town has a big food store.
14. The boy can not count to ten.

* Important: make sure your student says the sounds as (s)he writes.

Lesson 18

1. chew
2. blew
3. new
4. grew
5. stew
6. few
7. screw
8. would
9. should
10. could

11. The sun-flower grew in the soil.
12. The bird flew away.
13. The ship had a crew of ten men.
14. We found the loud sound.

Lesson 19

1. take
2. shape
3. hide
4. plate
5. frame
6. snail
7. pain
8. float
9. loan
10. glue

11. This is the last week, before the play.
12. For snack, I had a cupcake.
13. I like to ride the train.
14. Make a wish on a shooting star.

Lesson 20

1. taking
2. shaping
3. hiding
4. tapping
5. sipping
6. staying
7. feeding
8. feeling
9. boating
10. playing

11. I was hoping we could meet later.
12. The sleeping chick woke up and found his mother.
13. Can we go camping this summer?
14. She is teaching us how to cook.

* Important: have your student read what (s)he wrote by sounding out the sounds, and then make the corrections..

Lesson 21

1. stopped
2. planned
3. hopped
4. ripped
5. tripped
6. slipped
7. lasted
8. lifted
9. jumped
10. lowered

11. She tricked me into doing her homework.
12. We shopped for a new car.
13. The girl clapped her hands.
14. We stayed up to see the blue moon.
15. I opened the can of beans for dinner.

Lesson 22

1. hand
2. find
3. kind
4. mind
5. spend
6. wild
7. child
8. under
9. thunder
10. cried
11. tried
12. landed
13. spending
14. sending
15. remind

* Important: make sure your student says the sounds as (s)he writes.

Lesson 23

1. tractor
2. fact
3. object
4. ejected
5. insect
6. strict
7. impact
8. October

9. The man inspected the new car by kicking the tires.
10. The brick house was constructed in three months.
11. The sick child went to see the doctor.
12. I did a project for my teacher.
13. I cannot predict what will happen.

Lesson 24

1. yawn
2. lawn
3. dawn
4. talk
5. walk
6. haul
7. fault
8. haunt
9. fall
10. stall

11. If you eat raw chicken, you may get sick.
12. The long hallway was haunted.
13. You must follow the law.
14. The man called to ask if the car was for sale.

Lesson 25

1. please
2. rose
3. loose
4. pause
5. because
6. before
7. false
8. house
9. mouse
10. horse

11. Close the door when you enter the room.
12. The girl had to choose her new outfit.
13. The noise came from the boy banging on the drums.
14. At dawn, the sun will rise.

Lesson 26

1. yesterday
2. party
3. myth
4. type
5. mighty
6. happy
7. witty
8. yummy
9. story
10. sticky

11. The tiny girl skipped to school.
12. The dog had floppy ears.
13. The girl took the candy from the jar.
14. It was a sunny day.

Lesson 27

1. louder
2. proudly
3. sloppy
4. sloppily
5. sloppier
6. happily
7. happier
8. luckily
9. luckier
10. softly

11. The girl suddenly got sick.
12. They really wanted to see the show.
13. Tim is funnier than Tom.
14. The sickly child felt better.

Lesson 28

1. age
2. large
3. edge
4. fudge
5. energy
6. change
7. charge
8. bridge
9. page
10. stage

11. You must wash the germs away.
12. The ink from the pen will smudge.
13. The judge sat on a high bench.
14. The broken down car would not budge.

Lesson 29

1. place
2. face
3. space
4. trace
5. race
6. dance
7. chance
8. pencil
9. ice
10. slice

11. Do not force me to jump off the branch.
12. What choice did I have?
13. I did not have a chance to say good-bye.
14. In the distance, we could see a sail boat.

Lesson 30

1. plastic
2. kite
3. magic
4. public
5. attic
6. pocket
7. ticket
8. topic
9. frantic
10. basic

11. You need to practice the dance.
12. We went to the park to have a picnic.
13. The story was romantic.
14. Take the hamster out of its cage.
15. The traffic made us late.

Lesson 31

1. dishes
2. boxes
3. houses
4. wishes
5. lashes
6. babies
7. ladies
8. stories
9. shirts
10. tickets
11. pockets
12. branches
13. loaves
14. wives
15. scarves

Lesson 32

1. spilled
2. wall
3. passing
4. grass
5. stuff
6. unless
7. most
8. dress
9. boss
10. off
11. fold
12. gold
13. roll
14. scroll
15. post

Lesson 33

1. total
2. allow
3. always
4. almost
5. alive
6. equal
7. animal
8. oval
9. alarm
10. moral

11. The dog jumped on me and licked my face.
12. The queen wore a crown.
13. She carried the backpack for over a mile.
14. We had a problem with the kitchen sink.
15. What is the moral of the story?

* Important: make sure your student says the sounds as (s)he writes.

Lesson 34

1. couldn't
2. wouldn't
3. haven't
4. didn't
5. weren't
6. she's
7. he'll
8. doesn't
9. don't
10. they're

11. I'll go to the store later.
12. You shouldn't go out after dark.
13. You'd like that story.
14. They'll see the show on Friday.

Lesson 35

1. to
2. too
3. two
4. there
5. their
6. they're
7. made
8. maid
9. hole
10. whole

* Words should be studied.

11. Their kitten jumped up and grabbed the string.
12. The two boys planned to meet under the bridge.
13. My father sent a letter to me.
14. The wind blew the leaves.
15. We ate most of the pie.

Lesson 36

1. knee
2. know
3. knew
4. knock
5. hour
6. climb
7. comb
8. numb
9. wrong
10. answer
11. what
12. when
13. which
14. while
15. white

* Words should be studied.

---

* At this point in the reading program, the dictations should become optional, since the words become much more difficult.
If you continue with the dictations, words may need to be studied first.

Lesson 37

1. relief
2. brief
3. brownie
4. belief
5. chief
6. cookie
7. eight
8. weight

9. The soccer field was wet from the rain.
10. I would like a piece of pie.
11. Tim is in eighth grade.
12. Jim took the cookie from the jar.

Lesson 38

1. dead
2. head
3. read
4. dread
5. bread
6. instead
7. ready
8. death

9. The chair was too heavy to lift.
10. The sweater was too large.
11. We found a feather on the beach.
12. The gray clouds were a threat to our picnic.

Lesson 39

1. special
2. social
3. socially
4. partial
5. partially
6. facial
7. official
8. crucial
9. confidential
10. initial

11. My teacher said that I have potential.
12. I felt special on my birthday.
13. Puppies are social animals.
14. The official rules were posted on the wall.

Lesson 40

1. action
2. lotion
3. addition
4. invention
5. condition
6. option
7. vision
8. invasion

9. I didn't like the motion of the waves.
10. We picked a location for our vacation.
11. My mother got a promotion at work.
12. Our nation has a large population.

* There are no dictations for Lesson 41

Lesson 42

1. radio
2. audio
3. zero
4. hello
5. pasta
6. America
7. taxi
8. also

9. We sat on the sofa and watched a movie.
10. My garden has a lot of tomato plants.
11. On Saturday nights, we always order pizza.
12. The hungry boy wanted a baked potato.

Lesson 43

1. puzzle
2. able
3. stable
4. cable
5. candle
6. bottle
7. little
8. angle
9. apple
10. people

11. The kitten liked to cuddle with the puppy.
12. The gymnast was flexible.
13. We were in the middle of the park.
14. Anything is possible, if you try hard.

Lesson 44

1. picture
2. future
3. nature
4. moisture
5. venture
6. culture
7. rupture
8. structure

9. James fell and fractured his arm.
10. You must stand tall for good posture.
11. The cows were grazing in the pasture.
12. She didn't like the texture of the wool pants.

Lesson 45

1. dangerous
2. nervous
3. famous
4. marvelous
5. humorous
6. numerous
7. timely
8. happily

9. The little kitten was curious.
10. The child had a virus and needed a doctor.
11. The dog pawed at the door.
12. The chicken laid numerous eggs.

Lesson 46

1. drive
2. leave
3. five
4. active
5. one
6. massive
7. positive
8. negative
9. never
10. selective

11. We mostly see our relatives on holidays.
12. Always strive to be your best.
13. The clever boy was very inventive.
14. In a crime, there is always a motive.

Lesson 47

1. chef
2. parachute
3. chord
4. stomach
5. chronic
6. mustache
7. chemical
8. mechanic

9. The sorry boy wanted a second chance.
10. If you shout out loud, you might hear an echo.
11. Don't let a small child use a sharp knife.
12. What is the solution to the problem?

Lesson 48

1. phone
2. phrase
3. dolphin
4. taught
5. caught
6. fought
7. bought
8. brought
9. daughter
10. enough

11. I caught a cold and got a cough.
12. I like to watch the dolphins do tricks.
13. We thought the woman was driving too fast.
14. The bully tried to act tough.

Lesson 49

1. magician
2. technician
3. loudest
4. nicer
5. ready
6. trying
7. following
8. friendly
9. knife
10. knives

11. On Tuesday we will go to the zoo.
12. The magician arrived for the party.
13. We have laws to limit pollution.
14. The girl ate a tuna-fish sandwich.
15. The panda bear comes from China.

Lesson 50

1. hour
2. honor
3. honest
4. group
5. soup
6. ballet
7. filet
8. sorbet

9. The ballet dancer stood on her toes.
10. The honest child never told lies.
11. We had mushroom soup for dinner.
12. For dessert, we had orange sorbet.

Blast Off to Learning Press

Check out our other reading programs for all ages!

Check out our other games and online tools!

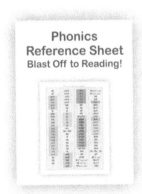

Phonics Reference Sheet
Blast Off to Reading!

Phonics BINGO

Flash Cards for
Blast Off to Reading!

Neighborhood Phonics

Phonics Reference Sheet
I Can Fly
Reading Program

Phonics Board Games

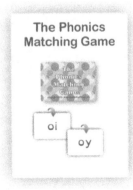

The Phonics Matching Game

The Silent 'e' Matching Game

CPSIA information can be obtained
at www.ICGtesting.com
Printed in the USA
JSHW040755200521
14950JS00005B/226